Gender and Diversity in the Workplace

*Dedicated to the memory
of my mother Zina Powell,
a wonderful parent and friend*

Gender and Diversity in the Workplace

Learning Activities and Exercises

Gary N. Powell

SAGE Publications
International Educational and Professional Publisher
Thousand Oaks London New Delhi

For information address:

 SAGE Publications, Inc.
2455 Teller Road
Thousand Oaks, California 91320

SAGE Publications Ltd.
6 Bonhill Street
London EC2A 4PU
United Kingdom

SAGE Publications India Pvt. Ltd.
M-32 Market
Greater Kailash I
New Delhi 110 048 India

Printed in the United States of America

Library of Congress Cataloging-in-Publication Data

Powell, Gary N.
    Gender and diversity in the workplace: learning activities and
exercises / author, Gary N. Powell.
        p.   cm.
    ISBN 0-8039-4486-1 (pb)
    1. Sex discrimination in employment.   2. Sex role in the work
environment.   3. Minorities—Employment.   4. Affirmative action
programs.   5. Reverse discrimination in employment.   I. Title.
HD6060.P69   1994
331.13'3—dc20   94-7488
                                                                          CIP

94 95 96 97 98 10 9 8 7 6 5 4 3 2

Sage Production Editor: Yvonne Könneker

Contents

Preface

The demographic composition of the labor force is changing around the world. In the United States, the proportions of both women and members of "minority" groups (African, Hispanic, Asian, and Native Americans and others) have steadily increased in recent years. More individuals who are demographically dissimilar from each other are working together than at any time since the Industrial Revolution. In response to these changes, many colleges and universities have initiated courses, and many work organizations have instituted developmental programs for managers, administrators, and other employees, on the topic of gender and diversity in the workplace. The purpose of this book is to provide a complete and comprehensive set of instructional materials that may be used to address this topic.

Various exercises have been designed to be used with many different audiences: graduate and undergraduate students in academic disciplines—such as business administration, psychology, communications, education, counseling, social work, public administration, and health care administration—and members of both business organizations and not-for-profit organizations in fields such as health care, social services, government, and education.

Over half of the exercises originated in the graduate course entitled "Women and Men in Management" that I have taught at the University of Connecticut for several years, including ones that I prepared specifically for the course and others that emerged from student projects. The remaining exercises were contributed by colleagues who have taught similar courses. Only about one quarter of these exercises have been previously published.

You will find a wide variety of types of exercises, including individual, group, and class activities, diagnostic instruments, role plays, case studies, and simulations. The book has been designed to be used in conjunction with my book entitled *Women and Men in Management* (2nd ed., Sage, 1993). It also may be used on its own or in conjunction with other books on gender and diversity in the workplace. Although many of the exercises were originally designed to examine male/female issues, most may be used to examine a variety of diversity issues in any kind of work setting. A separate instructor's manual provides guidance on how to run the various exercises, including how they may be adapted for special purposes.

As you participate in these exercises, you will gain a greater appreciation of the wide range of issues that arise when people classify themselves or are classified by others as members of different groups, whatever the basis for group classification may be. You should also gain a firm grasp of how these issues may be dealt with in a manner that preserves integrity and takes advantage of the potential contributions of all members of the workforce, regardless of sex, skin color, or other personal characteristics.

I wish to thank several individuals for their help with this book: Diane Adams for another excellent job of copyediting; Marquita Flemming and Harry Briggs at Sage Publications for their enthusiasm about this project and their wise counsel; Tiger the Cat for her loving, affectionate, and playful presence in my life; and Laura Graves, my wife and favorite colleague, for continuing to stand by (not behind) me and encourage me all the way.

When I Was Young

Purpose:	1. To examine the early experiences of women and men of different ages.
	2. To identify the ways in which sex role expectations have changed, as well as the ways in which they have remained the same, in recent years.
	3. To compare your own early experiences and the expectations that have shaped your behavior with those of others.
Preparation:	Conduct a personal interview as described below.
Time:	60 to 90 minutes

INTRODUCTION

When *I* was young, my grandparents, parents, and other elder family members liked to tell stories of what life was like when *they* were young. I wasn't that interested: The stories mostly confirmed my beliefs about how weird life had been in the past compared to how it was now. In fact, over time, "when I was young" came to be a catch-phrase that prompted the automatic response "Oh no, not again," at which point everyone would laugh.

The purpose of this exercise is to reverse the association that you may have, if your association is similar to mine, to the phrase "when I was young." Instead of avoiding the stories that typically accompany the phrase, you will be part of a group that seeks out such stories from men and women of different age groups. When you consider the different stories you hear about people's early experiences, hopes, fears, the expectations placed on them about their future work and nonwork lives, and their beliefs about how things have changed over time, you will have a richer sense of how sex role expectations and their effects on behavior have varied (or not varied) over the last half-century and how sex roles may have influenced your own early experiences.

INSTRUCTIONS

1. In a prior class, the instructor will have assigned you one of the following types of individuals to interview outside of class:

   a. a woman over 60 years old

   b. a man over 60 years old

   c. a woman in her 40s

   d. a man in his 40s

   e. a woman in her 20s

   f. a man in his 20s

   g. some other type of individual as specified

2. As you conduct your interview, jot down brief answers to the following questions:

   a. What was it like to be a boy/girl when you were young (say about 10 years old)?

   b. What did you *want* to do, considering both your work life and nonwork life, when you grew up?

   c. What did you *expect* to do when you grew up?

    d. What *constraints and opportunities* did you see, if any, on what you could do with your life because you were male/female?

    e. How do you think things have changed for boys/girls since you were young? Have things changed for the better or for the worse? Why?

    f. If you had the choice, would you rather be a young boy/girl now or when you actually were one? Why?

    g. Other responses:

3. In class, form groups of individuals who interviewed the same type of person (e.g., woman in her 40s, man in his 20s).

4. As a group, compare notes on the different interviews held and prepare a 5-minute report about the experiences and beliefs that are characteristic of the type of person your group interviewed. (30 minutes)

5. Each group presents its report. (5 minutes per report)

6. Participate in a class discussion based on the following questions: (remaining time)

    a. How have the experiences of young *girls* changed over the last half-century? How have the experiences of young *boys* changed over the same period of time? Are these experiences more similar or more different now than before?

b. How similar or different are the beliefs of individuals of different sexes and ages about what it is like to be young today? How do these beliefs compare with your own beliefs?

c. How were your early experiences similar to or different from those of others you have heard about in this exercise?

Your Personal Qualities

Purpose: To increase your awareness and understanding of the personal qualities that you bring to work settings.

Preparation: Complete materials provided by instructor.

Time: 60 to 90 minutes

INTRODUCTION

Everyone brings a wide variety of personal qualities or characteristics to the workplace. The personal qualities that *you* bring to work settings include your needs, motives, values, beliefs, and attitudes. Most of these personal qualities are unobservable by other people, unless you tell others what those qualities are or unless you act them out. However, other personal characteristics, such as sex and race, are directly observable by others. The latter characteristics may not influence how you react to work settings and the people in them, but they may influence how other people react to you.

In general, your personal qualities may have three types of effects on your experiences at work:

1. They may affect how you emotionally react to different kinds of work situations and people.

2. They may affect how you behave in the various work roles that you hold.

3. They may affect how others react to you as a co-worker, supervisor, or subordinate and how they behave in your presence.

5

The purpose of this exercise is to increase your knowledge of the personal qualities that influence your experiences at work by having you complete and score one or more self-assessment questionnaires. As you interpret your responses to these questionnaires and compare them with the responses of others, you will gain a better understanding of the personal qualities that make you unique.

INSTRUCTIONS

1. Complete the self-assessment questionnaires that are provided to you by the instructor.

2. Participate in a class discussion of how various responses to the questionnaires may be interpreted and what their implications are for behavior in work settings.

Stereotyping in Advertisements

Purpose: 1. To increase your awareness of how women and men are depicted in advertisements.
2. To identify elements of advertisements that do or do not reflect gender stereotyping.

Preparation: Prepare an advertisement as described below.

Time: 60 to 90 minutes

INTRODUCTION

Advertisements from magazines, television, newspapers, and other mass media convey messages about the roles that women and men play in the workplace as well as in the society at large. Until recently, ads rarely showed women in working roles and never showed them as executives. Several stereotypes of women's roles occurred regularly: (a) women's place as in the home, (b) women as not making important decisions, (c) women as dependent and in need of men's protection, and (d) men regarding women as sex objects, not as people. Women were most often portrayed as happy and diligent homemakers, beautiful and dependent social companions, or most concerned with being blond, being thin, or having other physical characteristics they did not possess.

AUTHOR'S NOTE: This exercise was prepared by Anne J. Burr, Deborah C. L. Griffith, David B. Lyon, Gertrude E. Philpot, Gary N. Powell, and Dorianne L. Sehring. It is reprinted from J. William Pfeiffer and John E. Jones (Eds.), *A Handbook of Structured Experiences for Human Relations Training*, Volume VIII. San Diego: Pfeiffer & Company, 1981. Used with permission.

Men have not exactly been portrayed in realistic terms either. For example, according to the world of advertising, men are always ready to drink beer, whether it is after they have overcome a physical challenge, such as driving cattle, or simply made it to the end of the workday ("For all you do, this Bud's for you"). Even advertisements for the same type of product make different appeals to men and women. The emphasis of jeans advertisements for men is on being an individual and doing one's own thing, whereas the emphasis for women is on enhancing one's appearance.

The purpose of this exercise is to make you more aware of the subtle and not-so-subtle messages in advertisements by giving you the opportunity to create your own advertisements and examine how your ad and the ads designed by others depict women and men at work.

INSTRUCTIONS

1. Prior to class, use the space below to prepare a one-page advertisement to appear in a popular magazine or newspaper specified by the instructor. The ad should promote the ease of using a coffeemaker and show one, three, or five people in a work setting.

2. In class, form groups of four to six members.

3. As a group: (30 minutes)

   a. Discuss the thoughts and concerns you had while designing your ad.

   b. Together, design a new advertisement to be presented to the class. This ad is to reflect members' views on the most effective approach to use in selling the product.

4. Each group presents its ad and the rationale for it. (15 minutes)

5. Participate in a class discussion based on the following questions: (remaining time)

   a. How do the ads presented *reinforce* gender stereotypes? How do they *contradict* gender stereotypes?

   b. What steps can people take to overcome their own perceptual biases and to counteract gender stereotyping?

   c. What steps could the mass media take to counteract gender stereotyping?

   d. Why or why not might the media take steps to counteract gender stereotyping?

Raising Elizabeth/Robert

Purpose: 1. To explore socialization forces that influence women's and men's aspirations, occupational choices, and successes.
2. To put these socialization forces into a personal context.

Preparation: None

Time: 90 to 120 minutes

INTRODUCTION Individuals make their own decisions about what kind of work they will do. No one is forced into one type of work or blocked from another. We live in a free country where individuals have the liberty to choose the role, if any, they wish to play in the economy. Right?

Right only in a restricted sense. Most people are free to direct their own lives. The government doesn't assign jobs to people; they choose jobs for themselves. However, people are influenced in their decisions about work by outside forces aside from their own capabilities. In particular, they are influenced by their upbringing and by the messages that have been conveyed to them about society's norms for what women and men should do with their lives.

The purpose of this exercise is to examine the socialization forces that play such a large role in children's upbringing and to see how different combinations of forces may lead individuals to end up in very different types of careers, whether paid or unpaid. In it, you will have the opportunity to prescribe the ideal socialization for someone to be successful at a particular role. In so doing, you should gain greater

AUTHOR'S NOTE: This exercise was prepared by Janet Lee Mills. It is reprinted by permission from *Beyond Sex Roles* (2nd ed.), edited by A. G. Sargent. St. Paul, MN: West, 1985. Copyright © 1985 by West Publishing Company. All rights reserved.

insight into how socialization forces have influenced you and the people around you.

INSTRUCTIONS

1. Form groups of four to six members.

2. Your group will be "adopting" either a baby girl named Elizabeth or a baby boy named Robert and charged with the task of "raising" Elizabeth or Robert. You will be asked to raise Elizabeth to be either a successful manager, a successful secretary, or a successful corporate wife; or you will be asked to raise Robert to be either a successful manager, a successful road construction worker, or a successful corporate husband. You will be planning Elizabeth's or Robert's life for the next 21 years and determining what his or her experiences will be. You should be guided by your beliefs about what skills, knowledge, and attitudes he or she will need to fulfill the future role successfully.

3. As a group, use the two worksheets that follow as a guide for your choices in how to raise Elizabeth or Robert. Do not feel compelled to fill every space in the worksheets. Prepare a 5-minute report for class presentation. (30-45 minutes)

4. Each group presents key aspects of Elizabeth's or Robert's family data and experiences in early childhood, childhood, early adolescence, and late adolescence. Group presentations are in the following sequence: Elizabeth and Robert as manager, Elizabeth as corporate wife and Robert as corporate husband, and Elizabeth as secretary and Robert as road construction worker, with brief comparisons of reports by the class after each pair. (5 minutes per report, 5 minutes of discussion for each pair of reports)

5. Participate in a class discussion based on the following questions: (remaining time)

   a. What types of roles were you socialized for?

   b. How are people socialized to perform certain roles, perhaps without the awareness that it is being done?

   c. How does socialization affect women's and men's aspirations and chances of success?

   d. What can we do or not do to avoid such socialization and to open up a variety of options for children of both sexes?

   e. What can we do to offset some of the negative aspects of our own socialization?

RAISING ELIZABETH/ROBERT WORKSHEET A:
FAMILY DATA

Socioeconomic class

Racial/ethnic group

Religious affiliation

Father's occupation

Mother's occupation

Nickname

Birth order

Number and sex of siblings, if any

Relationship with siblings

Relationship between parents

Father's role with Elizabeth/Robert

Mother's role with Elizabeth/Robert

Extended family

RAISING ELIZABETH/ROBERT WORKSHEET B:
EXPERIENCES

	Early Childhood (0-5 Years)	Childhood (6-12 years)	Early Adolescence (13-16 years)	Late Adolescence (17-21 years)
Toys, personal objects, gifts				
Clothes				
Schooling				
Other "lessons," learning experiences				
Play, other activities encouraged				
Vacations, travel				
Pets				
Car				
Peer relationships				
Dating, romance				
Marriage and children (dreams and reality)				
Important family activities				
Responsibilities to family				
Work experience				

Counteracting Group Stereotypes

Purpose: 1. To explore the ways in which members of different groups stereotype each other.
2. To counteract the stereotypes that two particular groups have of each other.
3. To improve communications and working relations between groups.

Preparation: Complete statements below.

Time: 60 to 90 minutes

INTRODUCTION

When members of different groups possess negative stereotypes of each other, they are likely to experience difficulty in communicating and working together well. One of the simplest and most powerful ways to counteract this can be simply to ask the two groups to articulate and share their stereotypes with each other and then jointly identify ways to move beyond them.

In this exercise, the two groups may be women and men, Whites and people of color, or any two groups that need to improve their working relationship and ability to communicate.

INSTRUCTIONS
1. In a prior class, the instructor will have designated the two groups to be formed for this exercise.

2. Prior to class, complete the following statements as many times as possible:

   a. I see myself as . . .

   b. I see members of the other group as . . .

   c. I think the other group sees members of my group as . . .

3. In class, form the two groups. Each group should have its own, preferably private, space in which to meet.

4. As a group, complete the following statements as many times as possible, recording your answers below and also posting them on newsprint, a blackboard, or transparencies so they may be shared with others: (15-20 minutes)

   a. We see ourselves as . . .

b. We see members of the other group as . . .

c. We think the other group sees us as . . .

5. The two groups convene and share their lists of statements, discussing them as necessary for purposes of clarification and understanding. Record the other group's statements in the spaces below: (30-40 minutes)

a. Members of the other group see themselves as . . .

b. Members of the other group see us as . . .

c. Members of the other group think we see them as . . .

6. The two groups jointly complete the following statement as many times as possible: (remaining time)

We can communicate and work better with each other by . . .

What's My Line?

Purpose:	1. To examine the relationship between personal characteristics and occupational choices.
	2. To examine expectations about others' occupational choices when presented with limited information.
Preparation:	None
Time:	60 to 90 minutes

INTRODUCTION

When we first meet a person, we often base our judgments about him or her on our stereotypes. As we learn more about that person from our own observations, from that person, and from other people, we should be less inclined to base our judgments on stereotypes and more inclined to rely on the information we have received. However, our judgments may still be distorted by personalized stereotypes and expectations that we hold based on our own unique experiences.

The purpose of this exercise is to examine the ways in which people develop expectations about the occupational choices of others. You will receive increasing amounts of information about six people who were interviewed for purposes of the exercise and be asked to predict their occupations at each stage of the exercise. Then we will examine how stereotypes may have influenced your judgments and those of others, whether consciously or unconsciously.

AUTHOR'S NOTE: This exercise was prepared by Lisa Bourget, Susan Douglas, Pat Funaro, Tom O'Shea, Gary N. Powell, Anna Raymond, Diane Scholan, and Tracy Scott.

INSTRUCTIONS   1. The instructor will provide you with information gathered from interviews with six individuals who work in different occupations. The information will be provided in three stages. After each stage, you will be asked to guess the actual occupation of each individual, choosing from the following list:

A. secretary

B. registered nurse

C. physical therapist

D. social worker

E. secondary school teacher

F. real estate sales

G. computer programmer

H. physician

I. lawyer

J. engineer

Use the What's My Line? Recording Sheet to record your selections after each stage and record the same selections on index cards that the instructor will give you. Record the *letter* of the occupation that you are predicting for each person rather than writing out the occupation; this will enable quick tabulation of results. Feel free to change a selection for an individual from stage to stage. However, do not go back and change your answers in earlier stages. Also, do not use the same occupation for more than one person at any stage.

2. Stage 1: Record your selections for the occupations of the six individuals, knowing only their names. Record your answers on the recording sheet and on the index cards provided by the instructor. (5 minutes)

3. Stage 2: Record your occupational selections again on the recording sheet and index cards after receiving general information on the six individuals from the instructor. (15 minutes)

4. Stage 3: Record your final occupational selections on the recording sheet and index cards after receiving further information about the six individuals from the instructor. (15 minutes)

5. Stage 4: Record the actual occupations of the six individuals given to you by the instructor.

6. The instructor will tabulate the responses. (10 minutes)

7. After the instructor presents a tabulation of responses, participate in a class discussion based on the following questions: (remaining time)

   a. What were the primary factors that influenced your occupational selections for individuals in the different stages?

   b. Did the information provided at Stages 2 and 3 enable you to make more accurate judgments than before?

   c. For those individuals for whom you selected the correct occupation, what characteristic or characteristics most influenced your decision?

   d. To what extent did stereotyping appear to influence your responses and those of others?

WHAT'S MY LINE? RECORDING SHEET

Instructions: At each stage, record the *letter* of the occupation that you believe each individual holds. Do not go back and change your choices at earlier stages.

	Stage 1	Stage 2	Stage 3	Stage 4 (actual occupation)
Robert				
Eileen				
Humphrey				
Nancy				
Gary				
Ann				

7

Legislative Assistant Wanted

Purpose:	1. To gain experience in interviewing and being interviewed.
	2. To explore the dynamics of the interviewer/applicant relationship.
	3. To examine how biases may influence the interview process.
Preparation:	Read background sheet.
Time:	90 minutes

INTRODUCTION Recruiters, personnel officers, and managers typically have little information on which to base their decisions to hire one job applicant over others. Decisions about which applicants to interview are generally based on resumes, which present some information about applicants' backgrounds and experiences but little about their personal qualities. Even when applicants are referred to organizations by personal contacts, accurate information about them is lacking because the individuals who refer them usually give glowing descriptions. When recruiting is conducted on college campuses, decisions about which applicants to consider further are based on interviews that last no more than 20 to 30 minutes. The recruiter is likely to have read the resumes of up to a dozen applicants in less than an hour at the beginning of the day. As initial screening devices, campus interviews are necessary for organizations to reduce the large number of applicants who could possibly be considered to a select few who will receive closer scrutiny. However,

---

AUTHOR'S NOTE: This exercise was prepared by Laura M. Graves and Charles A. Lowe.

these interviews lead to quickly formed impressions that present only blurred pictures of applicants.

When judgments about individuals are based on very little data, as is the case when organizations make hiring decisions, these judgments may be influenced by stereotypes. Stereotypes may be based on such factors as gender, age, race, ethnic group, class, religion, and geographical region of origin. The purpose of this exercise is to examine the interview process, paying close attention to how stereotypes and personal biases influence the outcomes of interviews.

INSTRUCTIONS

1. Prior to class, read the Legislative Assistant Wanted Background Sheet.

2. In class, half of the participants will play the role of interviewer, and the remaining half will play the role of applicant. Two rounds of 15-minute interviews will be held; depending on your role, you will either conduct two interviews or be interviewed twice. After each round of interviews, both interviewers and applicants will complete an assessment sheet about the interview. After the second round, each interviewer will decide which of the two candidates to hire and will personally deliver a job offer letter to the successful applicant and a rejection letter to the unsuccessful applicant. Thus, if you are an applicant, you will receive either two, one, or no job offers. The instructor will divide the participants into interviewers and applicants, assign two applicants to each interviewer, determine the order in which applicants are to be interviewed, and give each interviewer a job offer and rejection letter to be delivered later. (10 minutes)

3. Review the background sheet and prepare for your upcoming interviews as interviewer or applicant. (10 minutes)

4. Conduct the first interview. (15 minutes)

5. Complete the interviewer or applicant assessment sheet for the first interview. (5 minutes)

6. Conduct the second interview. (15 minutes)

7. Complete the interviewer or applicant assessment sheet for the second interview. (5 minutes)

8. Each interviewer decides which applicant to hire and personally delivers job offer and rejection letters. (5 minutes)

9. After the instructor has collected information from the class about the results of interviews, participate in a class discussion based on the following questions: (remaining time)

   a. How relaxed and spontaneous were the interviews?

   b. What are examples of particularly useful questions that were asked? Offensive or otherwise inappropriate questions?

   c. Did any questions or behaviors by interviewers reflect personal biases or stereotypes? Questions or behaviors by applicants?

   d. Did any interview decisions reflect personal biases or stereotypes?

   e. Did interviewers and applicants tend to make similar assessments of their interviews with each other?

   f. For interviewers, what feelings were associated with offering a job to one person and rejecting another? For applicants, what feelings were associated with receiving or not receiving a job offer?

   g. What are the implications of this exercise for how to conduct oneself in an interview situation, whether as interviewer or applicant?

LEGISLATIVE ASSISTANT WANTED BACKGROUND SHEET

Background: Dr. Pat Dooley is the head of the Legislative Research Office for the legislature of a state government. This office is responsible for developing projections of the impact of proposed legislation by senators and representatives on state revenues and/or expenditures. To do this, Dooley requires an up-to-date computerized model of the state's economy. He must be prepared to vary the assumptions of the model and have it assess the estimated impact of possible legislation on very short notice.

The Current Situation: Dooley is looking for a bright, energetic, and ambitious legislative assistant to be in charge of the computerized model. The pay is extremely good, and the exposure to the workings of state government is invaluable to anyone interested in a career in public administration. The assistant will be responsible for making sure that the model accurately reflects the state's economy and having the model ready to run at short notice. This will involve talking to economists and other experts about the state's economy, keeping aware of the spending and income patterns of state residents, and being able to communicate the essentials of the model and the effects of changing its assumptions to nonexperts (i.e., state senators and representatives). The assistant should be flexible, be able to get involved in new experiences, be able to adapt to immediate and specific circumstances, and be at ease with people.

Interviewer's Role: You are a senior legislative assistant who directly reports to Dooley. You have been asked to interview two applicants who have been identified through campus interviews at the state university and determine which of the two is best suited for the job. Both applicants will graduate shortly with a master's degree from the Public Administration Program and have similar internship experience and work experience (mostly part-time). Before the interview, consider what job-relevant skills you are looking for in an applicant, including whether his or her personality seems right for the job.

Applicant's Role: You will be graduating shortly with a master's degree from the Public Administration Program at the state university and would very much like the position in Dooley's office. You have already made it past the campus interview. Now you just need to do well in this interview to get the job. Put yourself in the frame of mind of someone who really wants the job. Before the interview, consider what skills you have that are relevant to this job and be prepared to make the interviewer aware that you have these skills.

LEGISLATIVE ASSISTANT WANTED INTERVIEWER ASSESSMENT SHEET

Interview With Candidate 1:

1. I got to know the applicant's skills and abilities.
   disagree   1   2   3   4   5   6   7   agree

2. I got to know the applicant as a person.
   disagree   1   2   3   4   5   6   7   agree

3. The applicant got to know what the job would be like.
   disagree   1   2   3   4   5   6   7   agree

4. The applicant got to know what this would be like as a place to work.
   disagree   1   2   3   4   5   6   7   agree

5. The applicant was able and willing to answer any questions.
   disagree   1   2   3   4   5   6   7   agree

6. The applicant tried hard to show interest in the job.
   disagree   1   2   3   4   5   6   7   agree

7. Overall, the interview went extremely well.
   disagree   1   2   3   4   5   6   7   agree

Interview With Candidate 2:

1. I got to know the applicant's skills and abilities.
   disagree   1   2   3   4   5   6   7   agree

2. I got to know the applicant as a person.
   disagree   1   2   3   4   5   6   7   agree

3. The applicant got to know what the job would be like.
   disagree   1   2   3   4   5   6   7   agree

4. The applicant got to know what this would be like as a place to work.
   disagree   1   2   3   4   5   6   7   agree

5. The applicant was able and willing to answer any questions.
   disagree   1   2   3   4   5   6   7   agree

6. The applicant tried hard to show interest in the job.
   disagree   1   2   3   4   5   6   7   agree

7. Overall, the interview went extremely well.
   disagree   1   2   3   4   5   6   7   agree

LEGISLATIVE ASSISTANT WANTED APPLICANT ASSESSMENT SHEET

Interview 1:

1. The interviewer got to know my skills and abilities.
   disagree   1   2   3   4   5   6   7   agree

2. The interviewer got to know me as a person.
   disagree   1   2   3   4   5   6   7   agree

3. I got to know what the job would be like.
   disagree   1   2   3   4   5   6   7   agree

4. I got to know what Dooley's office would be like as a place to work.
   disagree   1   2   3   4   5   6   7   agree

5. The interviewer was able and willing to answer any questions.
   disagree   1   2   3   4   5   6   7   agree

6. The interviewer tried hard to recruit me for the job.
   disagree   1   2   3   4   5   6   7   agree

7. Overall, the interview went extremely well.
   disagree   1   2   3   4   5   6   7   agree

Interview 2:

1. The interviewer got to know my skills and abilities.
   disagree   1   2   3   4   5   6   7   agree

2. The interviewer got to know me as a person.
   disagree   1   2   3   4   5   6   7   agree

3. I got to know what the job would be like.
   disagree   1   2   3   4   5   6   7   agree

4. I got to know what Dooley's office would be like as a place to work.
   disagree   1   2   3   4   5   6   7   agree

5. The interviewer was able and willing to answer any questions.
   disagree   1   2   3   4   5   6   7   agree

6. The interviewer tried hard to recruit me for the job.
   disagree   1   2   3   4   5   6   7   agree

7. Overall, the interview went extremely well.
   disagree   1   2   3   4   5   6   7   agree

Who Gets Hired?

Purpose:	1. To examine the criteria used by review panels to make decisions about candidates for a supervisory position.
	2. To examine how treatment and outcome discrimination may be manifested in the interview process.
Preparation:	Read background sheet.
Time:	90 to 120 minutes

INTRODUCTION

The introduction to the previous exercise, which has all class members participate in one-to-one interviews, applies to this one as well. In contrast, this exercise has review panels conduct interviews of two candidates playing specific roles. As a result, it gives us the opportunity to examine how having a review panel rather than a sole interviewer influences whether the interview process is characterized by *treatment discrimination* (discrimination in how the interviews are conducted) and/or *outcome discrimination* (discrimination in the final outcomes of the interview—i.e., who gets hired and at what salary).

AUTHOR'S NOTE: This exercise was prepared by L. V. Entrekin and G. N. Soutar. It is reprinted from J. William Pfeiffer and John E. Jones (Eds.), *A Handbook of Structured Experiences for Human Relations Training*, Vol. VI. San Diego: Pfeiffer & Company, 1977. Used with permission.

INSTRUCTIONS   1. In a prior class, the instructor will have designated two participants to play the roles of Harold Jones and Janet Oliver, the individuals to be interviewed, and 10 participants to serve on two 5-person review panels that will interview Harold and Janet. Review panels will be given a salary range for the open position. All other participants will act as silent observers, focusing on either Review Panel 1's two interviews, Review Panel 2's two interviews, Harold's two interviews, or Janet's two interviews.

2. In class, review the background sheet and prepare for interviews. Review panels should be in separate rooms if possible. Observers with a similar focus (Review Panel 1, Review Panel 2, Harold, or Janet) should convene to discuss what they will look for in interviews. (10 minutes)

3. *First round of interviews:* Review Panel 1 interviews Harold and Review Panel 2 interviews Janet. Review panel members record their impressions of the candidate on the review panel evaluation sheet. Observers record their impressions of the interview on the observer's sheet. (15 minutes)

4. Break between interviews. (10 minutes)

5. *Second round of interviews:* Review Panel 1 interviews Janet and Review Panel 2 interviews Harold. Review panel members and observers record their impressions as before. (15 minutes)

6. Each review panel decides (a) which of the two candidates to hire for the job and (b) what salary to offer the candidate, taking into account the salary range for the position. During this time, observers meet to share perceptions, and Janet and Harold meet to compare treatments by the review panels. (10 minutes)

7. Review panels announce their decisions and their rationale for making them. (10 minutes)

8. Participate in a class discussion based on the following questions: (remaining time)

   a. How was positive versus negative information about applicants used by the review panels?

   b. How did the two review panels differ in their general treatment of applicants?

   c. Was there any evidence of *treatment discrimination* in how the two candidates were treated by the review panels during interviews?

d. Was there any evidence of *outcome discrimination* in the hiring and salary decisions made by the review panels?

e. What are appropriate criteria to use in making such decisions? Inappropriate criteria?

WHO GETS HIRED? BACKGROUND SHEET

A large hospital is looking for a supervisor to oversee its Records Department, consisting of 15 female employees and a secretary. This department is responsible for filing patients' records and providing them to authorized hospital staff.

Jim Baker, the supervisor for the past 2 years, is being promoted, thereby creating the vacancy. He came into the position with a community college background. It is hospital policy to promote from within whenever possible. Two employees, Janet Oliver and Harold Jones, have applied for the supervisory position. Each knows about the other's application.

Janet Oliver is currently the secretary for the outgoing supervisor. She is 43 years old and has been in the department for 15 years, 10 as a clerical employee and 5 in her present position. She is thoroughly familiar with the requirements of the department and is considered an excellent performer. However, she can be abrasive, sometimes taking a "know-it-all" stance and, for some people, referring too much to her "vast experience" in the department.

Janet applied for the position at the time the current supervisor was hired. She was told that he was selected over her because of his superior background. Since then, she has obtained an associate degree in personnel administration at the local community college and is taking a course in supervisory skills there. Janet has told her friends that if she does not get the job this time, she will probably file a discrimination complaint with the regional office of the Equal Employment Opportunity Commission. However, she has no ambitions to rise above this job in the hospital's management ranks. She is the single parent of a teenage daughter who will graduate from high school next year and hopes to enter college.

Harold Jones is 23 years old and has a bachelor's degree in health care management from the state university. He has worked in the hospital's accounting department for 18 months and has obtained a thorough understanding of hospital operations. He has been an excellent performer in his position and is considered to have outstanding potential to rise further in the hospital's management ranks. However, Harold is considered an "operator" by some people and "wet behind the ears" and naive at times by others.

Harold sees the Records Department supervisory position as a significant step to a higher management position in which he could demonstrate his potential for positions at higher levels. Thus he does not anticipate spending more than 2 or 3 years in this position before moving up in the management ranks. He is married and the father of one preschool son.

WHO GETS HIRED? REVIEW PANEL EVALUATION SHEET

1. General impressions of your interview with Harold:

2. General impressions of your interview with Janet:

3. Which candidate do you believe is more qualified? Why?

WHO GETS HIRED? OBSERVER'S SHEET

1. Candidate observed: _____ Review Panel observed: _____

   General impressions of the interview:

2. Candidate observed: _____ Review Panel observed: _____

   General impressions of the interview:

3. What differences did you see in how the two interviews were conducted?

Entering a
Nontraditional Career

Purpose:	1. To examine what it is like for individuals to work in a nontraditional career.
	2. To develop ways of dealing with customers who are reluctant to accept employees in nontraditional roles.
	3. To observe superior-subordinate relationships when the subordinate is in a nontraditional career.
Preparation:	None
Time:	60 minutes

INTRODUCTION

When individuals enter a career that is nontraditional for members of their sex, they often have to deal with others who believe that they are not fit for the job. It is not easy to work with someone who is predisposed to consider you incompetent! The purpose of this exercise is to give you insight into the kinds of problems that individuals in nontraditional careers face and some ways in which these problems may be dealt with as they arise.

AUTHOR'S NOTE: This exercise was prepared by Christine S. Regula, Robert P. Cook, David W. Jourdan, and Gary N. Powell.

INSTRUCTIONS

1. Form groups of three members. Within each group, one person will play the role of a new employee of a service organization in a nontraditional career, one the role of a customer who deals with the employee, and the other the role of the manager of the employee.

2. Review the role description provided by the instructor. Prepare to act according to the guidelines for your particular role. Feel free to be creative in how you play your role and embellish it as you see fit, but also make it as realistic as possible. (5 minutes)

3. Conduct the role play. (maximum of 20 minutes)

4. Participate in a class discussion based on the following questions: (remaining time)

   a. What were your feelings about your assigned role?

   b. What were your feelings toward the other participants?

   c. Do you think that a similar situation could occur in real life? Why or why not?

   d. Was the conflict resolved? If so, how? If not, how might other behavior have changed the outcome?

   e. Were you satisfied with the resolution? Why or why not?

   f. Did issues of gender, race, or ethnicity enter into what transpired in your role play? If so, how were they dealt with by the various participants?

   g. What recommendations would you make to individuals in nontraditional career roles who find themselves in similar situations?

10

The Skyscraper Exercise

Purpose:
1. To examine factors affecting group decision making and performance on a task.
2. To examine gender differences in behavior in task-oriented groups.

Preparation: None

Time: 2.5 hours over one or two class sessions

INTRODUCTION

Members of a group may exhibit different types of behavior when they work together. One type is called *task-oriented behavior,* such as initiating, brainstorming, and generating possible solutions to a problem. A second type is called *social behavior* (or maintenance-oriented behavior), such as encouraging others in their expression of ideas, "gatekeeping" (making sure everyone has a chance to be heard), and reaching a consensus on the best solution to a problem. In most situations, both types of behavior are necessary for a group to be effective—task-oriented behavior to move the group closer to completion of its task in the short run and social behavior to preserve group harmony in the long run. The purpose of this exercise is to observe groups in action as they work on a task that has a concrete and well-defined objective.

AUTHOR'S NOTE: This exercise was prepared by Susan M. Schor and Gary N. Powell.

INSTRUCTIONS

1. Form groups of four to six members.

2. As a group, your goal is to build a "skyscraper" (i.e., the tallest possible structure) from a set of Tinkertoy[1] pieces or other building materials that the instructor will give you. You will have *25 minutes* to plan how you build your structure and *1 minute* to build it. The structure must stand on its own without falling for 1 minute after it is built. During the planning period, you can touch, count, sort, and try out how pieces fit together, but you cannot practice building the structure. The 1-minute building period will begin immediately after the planning period. As you work on this task, tape your discussion using a tape recorder provided by the instructor; as an alternative, your group may be videotaped as you work on the task.

3. Planning period. (25 minutes)

4. Building period, including measurement of height of various groups' structures. (5 minutes)

5. Participate in a class discussion based on the following questions: (30 minutes)

    a. What kinds of task-oriented and social behavior were exhibited during this task?

    b. Did any group members specialize in task-oriented or social roles?

    c. Were any group members more influential than others in their groups? What did they do to make themselves influential?

6. The instructor will provide instructions for additional stages of the exercise, which will involve either listening to the audiotape or watching the videotape of your group's planning and building period.

NOTE

1. Tinkertoy is a registered trademark of the Questor Corporation.

11

Communication Styles

Purpose:	1. To examine personal communication styles.
	2. To examine the influence of situational factors on individuals' choice of communication style.
Preparation:	Complete questionnaire.
Time:	60 minutes

INTRODUCTION
In her best-selling book, *You Just Don't Understand*, Deborah Tannen (1990) likened conversation between women and men to cross-cultural communication. She sees women and men as developing basically different communication styles in childhood and carrying these styles essentially unchanged into adulthood.

How do our own communication styles influence how we respond to others in work settings? We may be influenced by our childhood experiences, but we are also likely to be influenced by (a) norms about what kinds of topics are appropriate and inappropriate to discuss in the workplace and (b) our relationship with the person with whom we may discuss a given topic. The purpose of this exercise is to examine both personal and situational influences on how we communicate with others at work.

AUTHOR'S NOTE: This exercise was prepared by Diana J. Brooks, Andrea V. D'Agostino, Anne M. Farrelly, Victoria J. Greene, Robert P. Jeong, Gary N. Powell, and Patricia Wu.

INSTRUCTIONS
1. Prior to class, complete the questionnaire that follows.

2. In class, score your responses to the questionnaire on the scoring sheet provided by the instructor.

3. Interpret your scores according to the information sheet also provided.

4. Participate in a class discussion based on responses to the questionnaire.

REFERENCE
Tannen, D. (1990). *You just don't understand: Women and men in conversation.* New York: William Morrow.

COMMUNICATION STYLES QUESTIONNAIRE

DIRECTIONS: The following paragraphs describe various situations that could arise at work, each followed by three possible responses to the situation. Please circle the choice that seems most like the way you or someone like you would probably respond in the given situation.

1. Every year, your company grants a scholarship to an outstanding employee for enrollment in a full-time graduate degree program. The scholarship consists of full tuition and expenses, plus half of the employee's salary while in graduate school. Bill and Lorie both graduated with high honors from their respective colleges 3 years ago and have been working in the same department since. They are both considered great assets to the company. Now both are considering whether to apply for the scholarship. Lorie has asked you, as a co-worker, for your opinion about the merits of her competing with Bill for the scholarship. You reply:

   a. It will be interesting to see who they pick.

   b. I don't think you should get your hopes up—who knows how they will pick the winner?

   c. Lorie, you have been getting great reviews. You are definitely a great applicant for it.

2. Susan has just lost a major account with one of the firm's largest customers. You are the vice president of sales and have been informed that the major reasons were Susan's lack of preparation and initiative during the account renewal stage. Susan has been with the company for a year and usually performs well. She has asked to discuss the situation with you. She starts out by saying, "I want to explain what happened . . . " You reply:

   a. Susan, I can't understand what happened. You really didn't do your job.

   b. Yes, I think we need to figure out how to prevent this kind of thing in the future. What happened? This isn't like you.

   c. Okay.

3. You are the top operating officer at your company. Sid Jones, corporate travel manager, has just completed a presentation to senior management describing ways to save on corporate travel expenses. He has asked for approval of a controversial change in travel policy but has provided a good analysis of why the change makes sense. Sid has been with the company for only a year but has a solid record of accomplishment so far. You reply:

   a. Thank you, Sid, for your recommendations. We'll get back to you.

   b. It sounds like you ought to move ahead with this and make it happen! You've done a good job here.

   c. Let's not do anything until all of you have had a chance to review the proposed change with your departments. There may be other implications we haven't thought of. Sid, don't do anything further on this for now.

4. Michelle, your co-worker, has just been caught drinking on the job. You have heard rumors that Michelle is having family problems and know that her job is on the line. You want to help Michelle but aren't quite sure how to go about it. Michelle returns to her desk saying, "I don't know what I am going to do." She seems to want to talk. You reply:

   a. The boss looks mad, that's for sure.

   b. I don't know, but you'd better get your act together fast or you'll be in big trouble.

   c. Michelle, maybe you should call the Employee Assistance Program and get some professional help.

5. You go to the coffee machine one morning and run into one of your subordinates, Virginia. You extend a greeting and walk back to the office area together chatting about the weather, news headlines, and so on. All of a sudden, Virginia starts talking rather explicitly about how hard she and her husband have been trying to have children, stating, "I'm 37 and the clock is ticking." You reply:

   a. I can tell this is very important to you. Would you like to come into my office and discuss it further?

   b. That seems to be a common problem these days.

   c. I feel this is too personal a subject for me to be involved with. Why don't we get back to work?

6. Sal, a middle-level manager at the same level as you, is writing a report for his boss. This report must compile information from a number of departments within the organization. Sal may either spend time researching the required information, or he may more easily obtain it from department heads like yourself. Sal explains the project he is working on and asks, "Would you be able to provide me with the information I need by tomorrow? I would really appreciate your help. It would save me lots of time." You know that Sal is in a crunch, but he always seems to wait until the last minute. You reply:

   a. Sal, are you trying to pawn your work off again?

   b. Sure, it's no problem for me to put that information together for you. I'll have it to you tomorrow.

   c. I'll see what I can do.

7. You and Joe are middle-level managers in separate departments of the same organization. Joe is friendly with several of the vice presidents, and he works in one of the more influential departments. You are newer than Joe in the company. Joe meets you in the hallway one evening, when most employees have already left for the day. After a short humorous conversation about the day's events, Joe asks, "Are you in a hurry to get home? Do you want to go for a drink?" You reply:

   a. Sure, it will give us a good chance to talk.

   b. Sorry, I've gotta get going. See you tomorrow.

   c. That sounds like fun, but I've really got to work late tonight at home.

8. "What more can I say? You've heard our proposal. Our price and service are competitive, and you have received good feedback on us from other customers." Mary Anderson, senior sales rep for a major insurance company, is trying to close the sale on property insurance for your company. You are the risk manager, and your account would be a large piece of new business for Mary. You like the deal but aren't so sure about Mary. She seems overly aggressive, but maybe she's just an ambitious sales type. You reply:

   a. Thank you for your proposal. I'll put it on the Insurance Committee's Friday agenda.

   b. Well, that may be true, but I don't care for the pressure you're exerting to close this deal. You'll just have to wait until our Insurance Committee meets on Friday.

   c. Well, I like the program you've laid out, and your company's reputation is solid. You've certainly presented a strong case. I'm going to recommend approval to the Insurance Committee on Friday.

9. Robert and Diane are both software specialists with promising careers in your company. They have been married for 8 years and had their second child a year ago. When there was just one child to send to the day care center, they figured there was still an advantage with both of them working, and Diane returned to her job soon after the baby's birth. However, now with two children, they figure they will be better off if one of them stays home and takes care of the children. They have discussed this matter and have decided that Robert will be the one who stays home. As his immediate supervisor, your reply to Robert is . . .

   a. This is really going to hurt your career in the long term, even if you do decide to come back later.

   b. Robert, you are a valuable worker, and it will be hard to replace you. Please let me know when you are ready to return to work, and we will be glad to have you back.

   c. Okay. (Then you place a want ad for the position in Sunday's paper.)

10. You are the head of a procurement department for a major corporation. Because of the complexity of federal regulations in your area of work, you sometimes seek advice on contract clauses from an outside consulting service. One clause in a large contract currently being negotiated has been giving you particular concern, and you have discussed it several times with the consultant contact, Madeline Bennett. However, there has recently been a reorganization at the consulting service, and Mike Sanders has been put in charge of your account. After asking his opinion, you are told, "I have looked this clause over thoroughly. Based on the available data, I have no objection to inserting it in the contract." This opinion is completely opposite to Madeline's previous analysis. You reply:

   a. It sounds like you have a different opinion than Madeline did. Could you explain your reasoning in a little more detail so that I can understand why?

   b. Thanks for your opinion.

   c. That's not the way Madeline saw it. Why don't you talk to her and get her reasoning. I don't see how your opinion could be so different from hers.

12

The Taming of the Skew

Purpose:
1. To examine the internal dynamics of groups with subgroups of different sizes and composition.
2. To examine how the dynamics of groups vary as they work on different tasks.
3. To increase awareness of the types of behavior exhibited in group settings.

Preparation: Read background sheet.

Time: 90 to 120 minutes

INTRODUCTION

Based on her examination of work relationships in a large corporation, Rosabeth Kanter (1977; Kanter with Stein, 1980) identified four types of groups with different subgroup ratios that can exist in work settings. Although Kanter focused her analysis on small groups, which could be either work groups or groups of individuals who hold the same job, her analysis can be extended to groups of all sizes. Also, although Kanter focused on relationships between women and men in groups, her analysis can be extended to any group that has two distinct subgroups based on some other personal characteristic such as race, ethnicity, religion, age, and so on. For convenience, she called the members of one subgroup "Xs" and the members of the other subgroup "Os"; when there is an imbalance in the size of subgroups, the Xs are in the majority and the Os are in the minority.

AUTHOR'S NOTE: This exercise was prepared by Paul Boiano, Joanne Fitzgerald, Donna Hoh, Patricia Muldoon, and Gary N. Powell.

Uniform groups, consisting of all Xs, represent one extreme. *Balanced* groups, consisting of approximately equal numbers of Xs and Os, represent the other extreme. Between these two extremes are *skewed* and *tilted* groups. Skewed groups have a ratio of Xs to Os ranging from about 85:15 to almost 100:0. Tilted groups have less of an abundance of Xs over Os, with the ratio ranging from about 65:35 to about 85:15. The purpose of this exercise is to examine the effects of groups having different subgroup ratios on how group members work together on different kinds of tasks.

INSTRUCTIONS

1. The instructor will form at least three task groups of five members and ask for three volunteers to act as scorekeepers. Other participants will act as observers. Task groups will compete with each other in the three tasks described on the background sheet.

2. The following is in preparation for the team competition: (30 minutes)

   a. Task groups should select team members to compete in individual events within 5 minutes and then devote the remainder of the time to preparation for the individual events.

   b. Observers should meet separately to discuss what types of behavior to look for in the exercise.

3. Conduct Banner and Cheer Presentations and applause vote. (15 minutes)

4. Conduct Athletic Event. (10 minutes)

5. Conduct Question and Answer Event. (15 minutes)

6. Participate in a class discussion based on the discussion questions that will be distributed by the instructor. (remaining time)

REFERENCES

Kanter, R. M. (1977). *Men and women of the corporation*. New York: Basic Books.
Kanter, R. M., with Stein, B. A. (1980). *A tale of "O": On being different in an organization*. New York: Harper & Row.

THE TAMING OF THE SKEW BACKGROUND SHEET

Several task groups will be participating in a team competition. The competition will consist of three events: the Banner and Cheer Presentation, the Athletic Event, and the Question and Answer Event. Teams are to assign participants to each event *with no overlap*. The ultimate goal is to score more points than the other teams and win the overall competition. Teams will have 30 minutes to select participants for each event and to prepare for the competition.

Event 1:
Banner and Cheer Presentation

Select two team members who will be responsible for developing the team banner and cheer. These two people must completely design and draw the banner, compose the team cheer, and train the team in its cheer during the 30-minute preparation period. Teams will have 3 minutes to present their banner and cheer at the beginning of the competition. Team presentations will be judged on originality, creativity, and enthusiasm. After all teams have completed their presentations, an applause vote will be taken and the order of finish will be based on the scorekeepers' judgment of applause levels for each presentation. Only participants who are not on any task group and not serving as scorekeepers should applaud. Points will be assigned as follows: 1st place is 30 points, 2nd place is 20 points, and 3rd place is 10 points.

Event 2:
Athletic Event

Select two team members to compete in a basketball shooting contest. One team member will be the shooter and the other will be the rebounder/passer. The object is to score as many baskets as possible in a 3-minute period. Shots must be taken from behind a 10-foot "foul line" and will be worth 2 points each. You may practice for this event during the preparation period. Teams will shoot baskets simultaneously in different locations.

Event 3:
Question and Answer Event

Select one team member to compete against a contestant from each of the other teams in the Question and Answer Event (a contest similar to the *Jeopardy* television program). Questions will be asked randomly from each of three categories: Cooking & Fashion, Arts & Entertainment, and Sports. Each correct answer will be awarded 10 points. However, each incorrect answer will *cost* 5 points. The first contestant to raise his or her hand after the question is asked will be allowed to answer. If the answer is incorrect, the next remaining contestant to raise his or her hand will be allowed to answer, with the same reward for a right answer or penalty for a wrong answer.

The Winner

The team with the most cumulative points at the end of the three events will be declared the winner of the team competition.

People Like Us

Purpose:	1. To apply concepts of intergroup dynamics to everyday problems that people face.
	2. To develop an awareness of the underlying emotional dynamics that affect people's behavior when they hold minority or majority status in a group.
Preparation:	None
Time:	90 to 120 minutes

INTRODUCTION

A great deal of our self-concept and sense of identity comes from the groups to which we belong. This begins with our earliest socialization into the first group we ever belong to—our family. It continues as we become members of other groups, such as religious groups, Cub Scouts or Brownies, gangs, recreational leagues, political action groups, and so on. Throughout our lives, membership in something called "an identity group" has perhaps the strongest effect on our self-concept. Identity groups may be based on such personal characteristics as race, ethnicity, gender, sexual preference, and age or on shared experiences such as religion, political affiliation, educational programs, fraternities or sororities, and military service. Being male has a different impact on a person's sense of self-identity than being female. Being Black is a different experience from being White. Being gay affects a person's self-concept differently than being straight. In general, most people find that they are more comfortable when they are around people from

AUTHOR'S NOTE: This exercise was prepared by Judith A. Neal.

51

the same identity group than when they are "token" members of a group; this can have a profound effect on their productivity and commitment to work as well as on their feelings of satisfaction. The purpose of this exercise is to examine the identity groups of participants and how membership in their particular identity group affects the shared experiences of all group members.

INSTRUCTIONS

1. The instructor will guide participants in the formation of discussion groups based on their primary identity characteristics.

2. As a group, answer the following question: "What are the primary problems that people like us experience in this organizational setting?" Write down the three problems that bother you the most as a group. (30 minutes)

3. The instructor will provide instructions for further stages of the exercise.

Dealing With Sexually Oriented Behavior

Purpose:	1. To examine personal reactions to workplace situations with sexual overtones.
	2. To examine personal and legal definitions of sexual harassment.
Preparation:	Complete questionnaire.
Time:	´60 minutes

INTRODUCTION

Sexual harassment may be generally defined as the directing of unwelcome sexual attention by one individual toward another. When it occurs in the workplace, it has potential legal ramifications. In recent years, because of incidents such as those involving Professor Anita Hill and U.S. Supreme Court Justice Clarence Thomas as well as the Tailhook Association Convention, sexual harassment has become a highly charged public issue as well. Most people recognize that a line needs to be drawn between acceptable and unacceptable sexually oriented behavior in the workplace. However, the question remains as to exactly what types of behavior constitute sexual harassment. In other words, where should the line be drawn?

The U.S. Equal Employment Opportunity Commission (EEOC) ruled in 1980 that sexual harassment would be considered an unlawful employment practice under Title VII of the 1964 Civil Rights Act. It defined sexual harassment as "unwelcome sexual advances, requests for favors, and other verbal or physical conduct of a sexual nature"

AUTHOR'S NOTE: The questionnaire used in this exercise is modified and reprinted by permission of *Harvard Business Review.* An exhibit from "Sexual Harassment: Some See It . . . Some Won't" by E. G. C. Collins and T. B. Blodgett (March/April 1981). Copyright © 1981 by the President and Fellows of Harvard College; all rights reserved.

when submission to or rejection of the conduct enters into employment decisions and/or the conduct interferes with work performance or creates a hostile work environment (U.S. EEOC, 1981). When the ruling was issued, the EEOC correctly anticipated that its definition of sexual harassment would be regarded by many as too vague and in need of clarification. Others were left to interpret exactly what conduct is meant by it and when such conduct violates the EEOC guidelines.

The U.S. Supreme Court generally upheld the EEOC guidelines in 1986 in *Meritor Savings Bank vs. Vinson*, the first case of sexual harassment it considered. It concluded that two types of harassment are actionable under Title VII. In *quid pro quo* harassment, sexual activity is requested as a condition for gaining a job, promotion, raise, or some other job benefit. In *hostile environment* sexual harassment, one employee makes sexual requests, comments, looks, and so on toward another employee and thereby creates a hostile environment in which that employee must work, even when no economic benefits are lost as a result. However, the Supreme Court failed to define exactly what constitutes a hostile work environment (Koen, 1990).

Given the uncertainty over what legally constitutes sexual harassment, individuals' own definitions assume considerable importance in determining the sexually oriented behaviors that they feel entitled to initiate and their responses to behaviors initiated by others. The purpose of this exercise is to examine how personal and legal definitions of sexual harassment may be applied to different kinds of workplace situations.

INSTRUCTIONS

1. Complete the questionnaire that follows.

2. Participate in a class discussion based on the following questions:

   a. How would *you* respond in each situation?

   b. How do you think *most people* would respond in each situation?

   c. In which situations did sexual harassment occur according to your own personal definition of sexual harassment? According to the EEOC guidelines?

REFERENCES

Koen, C. M., Jr. (1990, August). Sexual harassment claims stem from a hostile work environment. *Personnel Journal*, pp. 88-99.

U.S. Equal Employment Opportunity Commission. (1981). Guidelines on discrimination because of sex. In U.S. Merit Systems Protection Board, *Sexual harassment in the federal workplace: Is it a problem?* (pp. E9-E10). Washington, DC: U.S. Government Printing Office.

DEALING WITH SEXUALLY ORIENTED BEHAVIOR QUESTIONNAIRE

INSTRUCTIONS: Circle all responses that apply in each situation. You may circle more than one.

1. As president of your company, you walk into the office of the sales manager to congratulate him on setting a new record in sales. When you enter the office, you find the sales manager standing very close to his secretary. She looks upset and flustered. What would *you* do about the incident?

   a. Nothing, not knowing what actually happened.

   b. Nothing, not wanting to confront the sales manager on a personal matter such as this.

   c. Talk to the secretary about what happened.

   d. Suggest to the sales manager that even the appearance of sexual behavior is unwise.

   e. Express strong disapproval to the sales manager and inform him that if such behavior continues, it will have an adverse effect on his career.

   f. Other:

   What do you think *most company presidents* would do?

2. You enter an elevator with another middle-level executive of the same sex. That executive stares at the body of the other occupant of the elevator, a lower-level employee of the opposite sex, for a few seconds and then winks in amusement at you. You see that the employee has noticed the attention. What would *you* do?

   a. Share that executive's amusement.

   b. Remain silent, believing that it's up to the employee to raise an objection.

   c. Remain silent because it's an embarrassing issue to raise.

   d. Indicate disapproval by your coolness or aloofness.

   e. Express disapproval within the employee's hearing.

    f. Express disapproval when you and the other executive are alone.

    g. Other:

What do you think *most executives* would do in this position?

How would your response differ if the employee *had not noticed* the attention?

3. An assistant vice president is one of the most promising executives in your company. He complains to you, the executive vice president in charge of his division, that his boss has been making unwelcome and persistent sexual advances. You have a private conversation with his boss, who insists that the AVP has mistaken her "innocent" remarks and gestures. What would *you* do?

    a. Wonder about the AVP's ability to handle interpersonal relationships.

    b. Advise the AVP on how he might better deal with such behavior.

    c. Offer the AVP a transfer to another division.

    d. Caution his boss against engaging in behavior that might be construed as sexual harassment.

    e. Express strong disapproval to his boss and inform her that if such behavior continues, it will have an adverse effect on her career.

    f. Other:

What do you think *most executive vice presidents* would do?

4. A junior administrator in a large hospital has been the object of persistent sexual advances from a doctor who works for the health maintenance organization that is one of the primary users of the hospital's facilities. She has tried to discourage these advances tactfully but has been unsuccessful. The woman brings her problem to you, the chief hospital administrator. What would *you* do?

   a. Offer to transfer the woman to a department in which she would be unlikely to have frequent contact with the doctor.

   b. Encourage the woman to keep trying to parry the advances without offending the doctor.

   c. Encourage the woman to be tactful but firm regardless of the consequences.

   d. Indicate your disapproval to the doctor.

   e. Inform a health maintenance organization administrator of the situation.

   f. Other:

What do you think *most chief administrators* would do?

Values Regarding Sexual Intimacy at Work

Purpose:	1. To identify a range of personal, ethical, professional, and organizational considerations related to sexual relationships at work.
	2. To examine the effect of such relationships on individual as well as organizational effectiveness.
Preparation:	Complete questionnaire.
Time:	60 to 90 minutes

INTRODUCTION   Sexual interest in a co-worker is not always unwelcome. In some cases, it is reciprocated and serves as the basis for an organizational romance between two employees. *Organizational romances* may be defined as relationships between individuals working together that are characterized by mutual sexual attraction and made known to others through the participants' actions.

Although most people root for lovers in principle because they like to believe that romantic relationships can have happy endings, organizational romances are controversial. Various observers have sharply disagreed over their merits and how they should be handled. The famed anthropologist Margaret Mead (1980) argued that, much like the taboos against sexual expression in the family that are necessary for children to grow up safely, taboos against sexual involve-

AUTHOR'S NOTE: This exercise was prepared by Peggy Morrison. It is reprinted from J. William Pfeiffer and John E. Jones (Eds.), *A Handbook of Structured Experiences for Human Relations Training,* Vol. VII. San Diego: Pfeiffer & Company, 1979. Used with permission.

ments at work are necessary for men and women to work together effectively. Eliza Collins (1983) recommended that both individuals be fired, or, if the more valuable person can still be effective, the other be fired.

Others have argued that people do not need protection or taboos but mutual respect for the freedom and rights of others, including the right to participate in an organizational romance (Horn & Horn, 1982). This right was defended by Mary Cunningham, who resigned from her position as vice president at Bendix in the early 1980s amid considerable media attention due to allegations of her having a romantic involvement with her boss, the company chairman, who had helped her career. (She subsequently married him.) Afterward, Cunningham stressed the value of romances that lead to marriage: "When a man and woman working in the same company cultivate a relationship that eventually leads to marriage, it enhances the couple's creativity as a unit" ("Statement by Mary Cunningham," 1982, p. A2) and helps the company's bottom line. Therefore, it would seem that organizational romances may benefit as well as hinder productivity.

Most individuals have to deal with both the need for intimacy and the need for accomplishment. Because the workplace is a convenient setting for meeting attractive people, individuals are frequently faced with situations in which they have to choose which need, if not both, they will fulfill. Although recognizing that romantic relationships pose problems for their organizations, people still have their own needs that may conflict, and must be reconciled, with the needs of the business. The purpose of this exercise is to examine participants' values concerning the positive effects of sexual intimacy at work, the desirability of managerial actions to discourage it, the acceptability of sexually oriented behavior in general, and the possibility of participating in an organizational romance themselves.

INSTRUCTIONS

1. In a prior class, the instructor will select at least three volunteers to prepare a skit to be conducted in front of the class.

2. Prior to class, complete the questionnaire that follows.

3. In class, observe the skit. (15 minutes)

4. Participate in a class discussion of issues raised by the skit and questionnaire, including the following: (remaining time)

a. Your personal reactions to the skit.

b. Your likely feelings and actions if you were the *supervisor* of either or both partners.

c. Your likely feelings and actions if you were a *co-worker* of either or both partners.

d. Your experiences related to issues raised by the skit, either as a participant or an observer.

e. Your conclusions about the influence of the relationship portrayed in the skit on the effectiveness of (1) the individuals involved, (2) co-workers, and (3) the organization as a whole.

f. Your responses to the questionnaire, which represent your values regarding the merits and appropriateness of workplace relationships involving sexual intimacy.

REFERENCES

Collins, E.G.C. (1983, September/October). Managers and lovers. *Harvard Business Review*, pp. 142-153.

Horn, P., & Horn, J. (1982). *Sex in the office.* Reading, MA: Addison-Wesley.

Mead, M. (1980). A proposal: We need taboos on sexuality at work. In D. A. Neugarten & J. M. Shafritz (Eds.), *Sexuality in organizations* (pp. 53-56). Oak Park, IL: Moore.

Statement by Mary Cunningham. (1982, May 8). *Hartford Courant*, p. A2.

VALUES REGARDING SEXUAL INTIMACY AT WORK QUESTIONNAIRE

INSTRUCTIONS: Select one number from this scale for each item:

> 1   strongly disagree
>
> 2   disagree
>
> 3   probably disagree
>
> 4   undecided
>
> 5   probably agree
>
> 6   agree
>
> 7   strongly agree

_____ 1. Sexual relations foster better communication between the workers involved.

_____ 2. Some sexual intimacy between co-workers can create a more harmonious environment.

_____ 3. When two workers cultivate a relationship that eventually leads to marriage, it enhances their creativity as a unit and helps their company's bottom line.

_____ 4. Management should take strong steps to discourage sexual propositions toward co-workers.

_____ 5. Supervisors who direct sexual attention toward their subordinates should be reprimanded.

_____ 6. Any worker who directs sexual attention toward another should be reprimanded.

_____ 7. Companies ought to ignore sexually oriented behavior between co-workers as long as it doesn't affect productivity.

_____ 8. It is all right for someone to look for a marriage partner at work.

_____ 9. It is all right for someone to dress attractively to draw the attention of co-workers.

_____ 10. I would be offended by a co-worker's flirting with the supervisor.

_____ 11. I would never get intimately involved with a co-worker.

_____ 12. I would never get intimately involved with my supervisor.

16

Intimacy or Distance?

Purpose: 1. To examine issues related to the management of interpersonal attraction in work settings.
2. To discuss the impact of the level of power held in the organization and the level of attraction felt toward the other party on interpersonal work relationships.

Preparation: Read Part 1 of the case.

Time: 2.5 hours over one or two class sessions

INTRODUCTION   As the number of women in management increases, the possibility of sexual attraction between men and women at work increases correspondingly. There are two important dimensions to consider when discussing situations involving interpersonal attraction: level of power (both formal and informal) in the organization and mutuality of interest in getting involved. These two dimensions suggest four types of relationships: ES (equal power, same levels of attraction), ED (equal power, different levels), US (unequal power, same levels), and UD (unequal power, different levels). Although there is some overlap between the four types in specific concerns that must be addressed to successfully manage the relationship, each presents a unique constellation of issues to be managed.

AUTHOR'S NOTE: This exercise was prepared by Duncan Spelman and Marcy Crary. It is reprinted from "Intimacy or Distance? A Case on Male-Female Attraction at Work," in *Organizational Behavior Teaching Review* (Vol. 9 No. 2, 1984, pp. 72-85). Used with permission.

This case, based on a real situation, involves parties who have unequal power in the organization and seem to have different levels of attraction toward each other (a UD relationship). It is structured as a five-part case. The parts will be distributed and discussed sequentially, calling on you to analyze what has happened thus far and to recommend what Barbara DiBella should do next. The unfolding of the story will provide a powerful means of highlighting the central issues of the case.

INSTRUCTIONS

1. Prior to class, read Part 1 of the case.

2. Participate in a class discussion based on the questions at the end of Part 1.

3. Read Parts 2-5 of the case as the instructor distributes them and then participate in class discussion of questions that will be raised after each stage.

INTIMACY OR DISTANCE? PART 1

Barbara DiBella began work in Spartan Corporation's management trainee program immediately after graduating from college with a major in marketing. Spartan had vigorously recruited her as part of its affirmative action efforts to increase the number of women in management positions. Although Barbara had work experience in summer jobs, this was her first full-time position. In the trainee program, Barbara would be assigned to various corporate departments for periods of 6 weeks to 6 months, so that she could receive an introduction to the complete scope of the organization's activities and also meet key people. While assigned to each department, she would be under the direct supervision of the department manager.

Paul Platowski was the corporation's marketing manager. He had joined the firm just 7 years ago, following completion of an MBA program, and had progressed very rapidly to his current position of power and prominence. He, too, had gone through the management trainee program, following which he had selected marketing for his initial permanent assignment.

As Barbara's training assignment to the Marketing Department approached, she became increasingly apprehensive. Her fellow trainees and graduates of previous years' trainee programs told her many stories of Paul's interest in and involvement with young women in the trainee program. Barbara heard of no fewer than three former trainees with whom the grapevine said Paul had been or was intimately involved. Two of the three had excellent positions in the Marketing Department, and the third was progressing quickly in one of the product groups. The grapevine also indicated that Paul had sought relationships with two other women trainees but had been rejected. One of these women was mired in an undesirable field sales job and the other had left Spartan.

The manager of the Accounting Department, whom Barbara did not know particularly well but to whom she was assigned just prior to her rotation through marketing, warned her to be careful of Paul. He said he wouldn't be surprised if top management had stalled the marketing manager's rise at its current level until he "cleans up his act."

Barbara was also concerned about her upcoming contact with Paul because he seemed to always have his arm around women when he was with them in the halls, at lunch, and at social gatherings.

1. What is going on here?

2. What risks are there for Barbara in getting "involved" with Paul?

3. Are there any risks for Paul in getting "involved" with Barbara?

4. What would you do if you were Barbara?

Alternative Lifestyles Role Play

Purpose:
1. To identify the difficulties for individuals who lead alternative lifestyles.
2. To identify workplace issues raised by alternative lifestyles from the perspective of both individuals and organizations.

Preparation: None

Time: 75 to 90 minutes

INTRODUCTION

Most discussions of the advantages and disadvantages of organizational romances focus on opposite-sex relationships characterized by physical intimacy. The same advantages and disadvantages also apply to same-sex, physically intimate relationships. However, gay romances have an additional level of complexity. Many gay employees fear retribution from their employers and co-workers should their sexual preferences become known. Typically, because of homophobia in the workplace, individuals in gay relationships are forced to keep their romances and lives private. If unsuccessful at maintaining their privacy, they are likely to suffer additional negative consequences that heterosexual couples do not face. The purpose of this exercise is to examine the issues that gay workers face should their sexual orientation be revealed to others. These issues include the responses that such revelations may prompt in supervisors and co-workers and the strategies that may be used to deal with others' reactions.

AUTHOR'S NOTE: This exercise was prepared by Glenn E. Lu.

INSTRUCTIONS

1. In a prior class, the instructor will have selected at least five volunteers to prepare two skits to be conducted in front of the class.

2. In class, observe the first skit. (15 minutes)

3. Participate in a class discussion based on the following questions: (30 minutes)

    a. What conflicts did the subordinate face within the personal and the work relationships?

    b. How is the decision depicted in the skit likely to affect the subordinate's career?

    c. What alternatives were available to the subordinate?

    d. Did the subordinate make the right decision?

    e. What do you think the typical supervisor would do?

    f. What do you think the supervisor *should* do?

    g. What do you think would be the typical response of co-workers?

4. Observe the second skit. (10 minutes)

5. Discuss the same questions and compare responses to them for the two skits. (remaining time)

Promoting
Effective Management

Purpose:	1. To examine how expectations for managerial behavior are "gendered."
	2. To examine how these expectations may restrict managerial effectiveness.
Preparation:	None
Time:	60 to 90 minutes

INTRODUCTION

Managerial stereotypes need to be reconsidered. Much as the masculine stereotype has provided a model of the "good boy" and the feminine stereotype has provided a model of the "good girl," a managerial stereotype (influenced by the fact that most managers over time have been male) has provided a model of the "good manager." The overall proportion of female managers has increased considerably in recent years, but not much at the upper levels of the managerial ranks. Thus we have reason to wonder whether the stereotypes that people have of good managers have changed or remain the same. We also need to examine the relationship between stereotypes of good managers and what actually seems to make managers effective. The purpose of this exercise is to examine how managerial stereotypes compare with gender stereotypes and how they compare with beliefs about and experiences with effective managers in today's work environment.

AUTHOR'S NOTE: This exercise was prepared by Mark Maier. It is reprinted from "The Gender Prism: Pedagogical Foundations for Reducing Sex Stereotyping and Promoting Egalitarian Male-Female Relationships in Management," in the *Journal of Management Education* (Vol. 17 No. 3, 1993, pp. 285-314). Used with permission.

INSTRUCTIONS

1. As a class, generate as many responses as you can (at least 15-20) to this question: "To be maximally effective as a manager, what qualities or skills does someone need to possess?" The instructor will write down responses as they are called out. Copy the list of responses as it is generated on a separate sheet of paper, leaving room for left-hand and right-hand margins. (10 minutes)

2. Divide the traits listed into three groups: those that you consider most important (top one third), those that you consider least important (bottom one third), and those that you consider moderately important (middle one third). Using a 3-point scale (1 = *most important*; 2 = *moderately important*; 3 = *least important*), indicate the group in which you have placed each trait in the left-hand margin. Then fold under the left-hand margin so that your rankings are no longer visible. (5 minutes)

3. In the right-hand margin, indicate your "gender identification" of each trait in response to the following: "Suppose you asked 100 people on the street or at the local mall whether they thought _____ (Trait X) was more typical of men or women in our culture. How do you think a *majority* of them would respond: that Trait X is more typical of women in our culture, more typical of men, or equally typical of both women and men?" Now fold under the right-hand margin. (5 minutes)

4. Fold open the left-hand margin. The instructor will take a "straw vote" of all participants to establish a class ranking, determined by a clear majority of votes, of each listed trait as falling into the "most important" (top one third), "least important" (bottom one third), or "moderately important" (middle one third) category. Indicate the class ranking as MOST, MOD, or LEAST in the left-hand margin. (10 minutes)

5. Fold open the right-hand margin. The instructor will take a second straw vote for each trait to determine which sex, if either, it is most associated with. If the vote clearly indicates that Trait X is presumed to be more typical of men, place an M beside it (M stands for masculine, not male!) If the vote clearly indicates that Trait X is presumed to be more typical of women, place an F beside it. (F stands for feminine, not female!) If the vote does not yield a clear class preference, place M/F beside the trait. (10 minutes)

6. Participate in a class discussion based on the following questions: (remaining time)

a. Which sex, if either, is seen to possess a greater abundance of the qualities that are seen as important for managers to be effective? (Consider the class' gender identification of the entire list of traits in answering this question.)

b. Which sex, if either, is seen to possess a greater abundance of the qualities that are seen as *most important* for managers to be effective? (Consider the class' gender identification of the traits ranked in the "most important" category in answering this question.)

c. To what extent have managers that you have actually worked for fit the profile of qualities seen as most important for managers to be effective?

d. What is likely to happen to a manager's effectiveness if he or she adopts exclusively masculine or exclusively feminine traits?

e. How does the list of qualities generated compare with the traditional masculine stereotype? With the traditional feminine stereotype? With the traditional stereotype of an effective manager?

f. What can you infer from the fact that few, if any, of the straw votes on the gender identification procedure were unanimous?

g. How may stereotypes of effective managers influence responses to actual managers?

h. How may stereotypes of effective managers influence individuals' choices about whether to pursue a career in management?

Management Training Program

Purpose:	1. To examine the relative desirability of specified personal traits for candidates for a management training program.
	2. To examine group decision making regarding candidates for a management training program.
Preparation:	Complete background sheet.
Time:	60 minutes

INTRODUCTION

The last exercise, "Promoting Effective Management," asked participants to generate a list of traits (qualities and skills) that a person needs to be an effective manager. This exercise uses a list of traits generated in such a manner as to examine managerial stereotypes further. Rather than asking about stereotypes of effective managers in general, it asks participants to choose between candidates for a management training program who possess different combinations of specified traits. The purpose of this exercise is to examine how the stereotypes that people have of effective managers influence their thinking about who should be encouraged to pursue careers in management.

INSTRUCTIONS

1. Prior to class, complete the background sheet as an individual.

2. In class, form groups of four to six members.

AUTHOR'S NOTE: This exercise was prepared by Thomas L. Ruble. It is reprinted from "Exercises in Sex Stereotyping and Androgyny," *Women and Men in Organizations: Teaching Strategies*, edited by D. M. Hai. Washington, DC: Organizational Behavior Teaching Society, 1984. Used with permission.

3. As a group, reach a consensus decision regarding how the eight candidates should be ranked and record it on the background sheet. Also record your group decision on newsprint or a blackboard as directed by the instructor. (15 minutes)

4. After all groups have posted their rankings, record the *total* of the rankings that each candidate received from all groups on the background sheet.

5. Participate in a class discussion based on questions that will be provided by the instructor. (remaining time)

MANAGEMENT TRAINING PROGRAM BACKGROUND SHEET

Your organization has announced openings for college graduates in its management training program. It is seeking high-potential graduates at both the bachelor's and master's levels to be trained for placement in supervisory and management positions. Any major is appropriate because the training program will be tailored to the interests, aptitude, and work experience of each trainee.

The organization is currently considering eight candidates. These candidates have already been interviewed on campus and are now being considered for a second interview. All of the candidates under consideration have good academic records and will graduate in the top third of their class. In addition, all have some job-related work experience, even if it is only part-time. Some information on the personal traits of each candidate is presented below. This information is based on evaluations by the campus recruiter and letters of recommendation provided by professors and previous employers.

The organization can invite only three of the candidates for a second interview. To help decide who to invite, you have been asked to rank order these candidates on the basis of the information provided. List your rankings in the Individual Ranking column, ranking your top choice as 1, your second favorite choice as 2, and so on down to 8 for your least preferred candidate.

Individual Ranking	Group Ranking	Name	Noteworthy Personal Traits	Total Rankings From All Groups
		Dan Adams	analytical, aggressive, willing to take risks, forceful	
		Joanne Block	tactful, active, aware of other's feelings, not timid	
		Mark Cooke	calm under pressure, grateful, outspoken, devotes self to others	
		Ken Davis	sensitive to the needs of others, understanding, friendly, sincere	
		Carol Evans	ambitious, willing to take a stand, strong personality, assertive	
		Sue Fisher	strong conscience, makes decisions easily, warm to others, worldly-wise	
		Bob Grant	self-confident, creative, outgoing, helpful to others	
		Janet Harmon	cheerful, mild mannered, compassionate, sympathetic	

Designer Paper Towers

Purpose:	1. To examine three roles that leaders typically play in organizations:
	a. as a leader of a group of subordinates working on a task
	b. as a representative of a group competing for scarce organizational resources
	c. as a maker of decisions about how to allocate scarce organizational resources
	2. To examine the behaviors that contribute to leader effectiveness in each of these three roles.
Preparation:	Bring old newspapers to the class period.
Time:	2.5 hours

INTRODUCTION

Individuals in managerial or leadership positions play several kinds of roles in organizations. They direct the activities of subordinates who are working on task assignments. They represent the interests of their subordinates in trying to gain access to scarce resources within the organization. In addition, they make key decisions about how the group or organization will proceed.

Most studies of managerial or leader behavior have examined two aspects of leadership style. The first, called *task style,* or emphasis on task accomplishment, refers to the extent to which the leader initiates work activity, organizes it, and defines the way work is to be done. For example, a manager who reorganizes a department, develops a description of the function of each department member, formulates department and individual goals, assigns projects, and gives details on how projects should be conducted may be considered high in task style.

The second, called *interpersonal style,* or emphasis on maintaining interpersonal relationships, refers to the extent to which the leader engages in activities that focus on the morale and welfare of people in the work setting. For example, a manager who expresses appreciation to subordinates for work performed well, is concerned about their job and work satisfaction, and seeks to build their self-esteem may be considered high in interpersonal style. Individuals' task and interpersonal styles of leadership are typically regarded as independent dimensions. That is, a leader may be high in both task and interpersonal style, low in both, or high in one but not the other. (The distinction between leaders' task and interpersonal style is similar to the distinction between group members' task-oriented and social behavior made in Exercise 10, "The Skyscraper Exercise.")

A third aspect of leadership style is the extent to which the leader exhibits *democratic leadership,* which allows subordinates to participate in decision making, versus *autocratic leadership,* which discourages such participation. Democratic and autocratic leadership are considered to be opposite decision-making styles.

The purpose of this exercise is to examine how these types of leader behavior apply to a variety of critical roles that leaders play in organizations.

INSTRUCTIONS

1. Bring as many old newspapers as you can to the class period.

2. The instructor will assign you to a four- to six-person group and designate the leader of the group. In addition, the instructor will designate one participant to serve as company president.

3. The assignment of each group is to respond to the following directive from your company president:

   Your project team has been asked to submit a proposal for a new "designer" product to be produced and sold by our company: designer paper towers. (I am sure that you are aware of the faddish success of other designer products: jeans, sheets, etc.) You will be competing with other project teams in the company to have your design selected. Only one design will be chosen. The primary criteria for design selection are conceptual appeal, attractiveness, and stability (towers should not fall over). Cost is a secondary consideration for now; cost is positively correlated with the popularity of designer products such that more expensive products are seen as more appealing products, up to a limit.

Each team will have 30 minutes to decide on a design and then 30 minutes to build a prototype unit from the materials available (newspapers, masking tape, and marking pens). Following the building period, I will hold a staff meeting with the leaders of all teams to review designs and decide which design, if any, will be selected. The team whose prototype is selected will be responsible for the final design of the finished product. Other teams will be disbanded and their members reassigned to other projects in progress.

4. As a group . . .

    a. Plan the design of your paper tower. (30 minutes)

    b. Build the prototype of the paper tower that you have designed. (30 minutes)

5. Complete Part A of the questionnaire. (5 minutes)

6. The president of the company will lead a staff meeting of the project team leaders. In the meeting, each team leader will present and defend the design of his or her group. By the end of the meeting, the president must announce a decision as to which design, if any, will be adopted. Nonleaders may observe the staff meeting but must remain silent during it. (30 minutes)

7. Complete Part B of the questionnaire. (5 minutes)

8. Participate in a class discussion based on the following questions: (remaining time)

    a. How well did the various project team leaders perform in directing their groups' planning and building effort? What leadership style did they exhibit in each of these phases? What leader behaviors were most effective? Least effective?

    b. How well did the project team leaders perform as representatives of their respective teams in the president's staff meeting? What behaviors by leaders were most effective in influencing the decision about which design to choose in their favor? Least effective?

    c. How well did the president perform in leading the staff meeting? Did the president exhibit an autocratic or democratic decision-making style? Which style do you think was the most appropriate?

d. Did the "best" design win the competition? Why or why not?

e. How did the fact that the specified criteria for selecting a design were entirely subjective influence behavior in the exercise?

f. What examples did you see of effective *follower* behaviors?

DESIGNER PAPER TOWERS QUESTIONNAIRE

INSTRUCTIONS: Use a 1 to 5 scale for all questions except No. 9, with 1 as *low* and 5 as *high*.

Part A: Complete Before the Staff Meeting

_____ 1. How satisfied are you with how you worked as a team during the planning period?

_____ 2. How satisfied are you with how you worked as a team during the building period?

_____ 3. How satisfied are you with the role you played in your team's work?

_____ 4. How do you evaluate the merits of your team's design?

_____ 5. How do you rate your leader in task style?

_____ 6. How do you rate your leader in interpersonal style?

_____ 7. How satisfied are you with your leader's performance so far?

Part B: Complete After the Staff Meeting

_____ 8. How satisfied are you with how your leader represented your team in the staff meeting?

_____ 9. Did the president exhibit a democratic or autocratic decision-making style in the staff meeting?

_____ 10. How satisfied are you with how the president handled the staff meeting?

_____ 11. How confident are you that the design chosen is in the company's best interest?

21

Culture Clashes

Purpose:
1. To examine the types of problems that managers face in working with individuals from different cultures.
2. To reduce your culture blindness by increasing your awareness of cross-cultural differences and how you react to such differences.
3. To develop your skills in dealing with people and organizations from different cultures.

Preparation: Read assigned role description(s).

Time: 45 to 60 minutes per role play

INTRODUCTION

"Culture clashes" abound in today's global economy. Managers at all levels are being challenged, many for the first time, to do a better job of dealing with peers, subordinates, bosses, clients, and business contacts from other countries. What we see today with regard to culture clashes may be just the tip of the interpersonal iceberg as we move into the 21st century.

The purpose of this exercise is to examine some of the problems that managers face when they cross cultural boundaries. Several role play scenarios are used, each of which is based on a real-life incident, to demonstrate the rich cultural diversity in approaches to business issues that exist around the world. Participating in these role plays should increase your knowledge and understanding of cultural differ-

AUTHOR'S NOTE: This exercise was prepared by John F. Veiga and John N. Yanouzas. Copyright by John F. Veiga and John N. Yanouzas at the University of Connecticut. Used with permission.

ences and sharpen your awareness of the impact of culture on business transactions.

INSTRUCTIONS

1. In a prior class, the instructor will form groups of three participants who will conduct up to three role plays. Each role play has two role players and an observer. The observer role should be rotated within the triad. You will be given a role description for each role that you will play in class. Prepare to play your assigned role when the time comes.

2. For each role play:

   a. If you are the role player in whose office the role play occurs, set up the meeting area by arranging desks, chairs, and so on.

   b. Conduct the role play. (20 minutes maximum)

   c. If you are the observer, observe the behavior of the role players. After the role play is completed, ask the role players questions such as these: (10 minutes)

      (1) Why did you behave the way you did?

      (2) What assumptions did you make about the other's culture? Why?

      (3) What perceptions do you now hold about the other's culture? Why?

      (4) How great was the culture clash between the two of you? Was it resolved? If so, how? If not, what behaviors kept it from being resolved?

   d. Participate in a class discussion based on the questions suggested for the observers, who will report the behaviors they saw. The cultural roots of these behaviors will then be examined. (remaining time)

This Is Your Life!

Purpose:	1. To examine the diversity that exists in people's work and nonwork life experiences.
	2. To examine the nature of the internal and external forces that influence people's lifelong experiences.
	3. To identify the key decisions made by you and by others for you that have influenced the course of your life.
Preparation:	None
Time:	90 to 120 minutes

INTRODUCTION

In *Alice's Adventures in Wonderland*, Alice, while walking through the woods, came upon a Cheshire Cat. She asked:

> "Would you tell me, please, which way I ought to go from here?"
> "That depends a good deal on where you want to get to," said the Cat.
> "I don't care much where—" said Alice.
> "Then it doesn't matter which way you go," said the Cat.
> "—so long as I get *somewhere*," Alice added as an explanation.
> "Oh, you're sure to do that," said the Cat, "if you only walk long enough." (Carroll, 1865/1962, pp. 87-88)

There are many influences, both external and internal, on how we "walk through" (run through, sleepwalk through, drift through, plan our way through, are pushed or coaxed through, etc.) our lives. Outside

AUTHOR'S NOTE: This exercise was inspired by an exercise by Alice G. Sargent in *Beyond Sex Roles* (2nd ed.). St. Paul, MN: West, 1985.

influences include parents, schools, colleges and universities, jobs, bosses, mentors, spouses or "significant others," and children; some internal ones are hopes, dreams, aspirations, expectations, interests, and abilities. Some we choose for ourselves, and others are chosen for us. In sorting out these influences, all of us grapple with the notion of "career" in some manner—what we want it to look like and what kind of balance we wish to achieve between our work and nonwork lives.

The purpose of this exercise is to examine what your career has been like and what you expect it to be like in the future. To facilitate matters, let's adopt a broad definition of career as *major activities, related or not related to work, that are of prime importance during one's life.* According to this definition, you have a career even if you are not engaged in paid employment or preparing for such employment, as long as what you are doing is important to you. This exercise is highly personal. It will remind you where you have been, where you see yourself going, and what has strongly influenced you along the way. It will also give you insight into how other people view their lives.

INSTRUCTIONS

1. On the next page, draw a "life line" for yourself, with ups and downs as appropriate. Time need not be marked off in constant intervals. Plot your life line up to the present, then continue by projecting how you expect it to look in the foreseeable future. The "high points" of your life line should reflect more positive experiences and the "low points" less positive experiences. Draw two lines if you wish, one for your work or student life and one for your nonwork life, and look at how they have influenced each other. Indicate the key events that have shaped your life line by using the symbols below, creating your own symbols where needed: (30 minutes)

!	where you took the greatest risk of your life
X	where you encountered an obstacle that prevented you from getting or doing what you wanted
O	where a critical decision was made for you by someone else
M	where a mentor or other key individual gave you critical assistance
+	at the point of the best decision you ever made
–	at the point of the worst decision you ever made
H	at the point of the hardest decision you ever made
?	where you see an important decision coming up in the future that either you will make or someone else will make for you

Write down what each symbol represents, either in a legend or along the line.

Here is a sample life line:

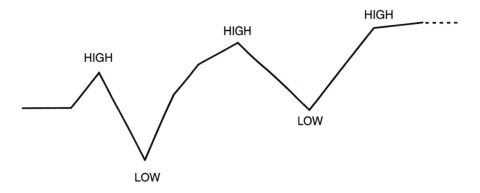

Draw your life line (or life lines) here:

2. The instructor will form discussion groups.

3. As a group, consider the following questions: (30 minutes)

    a. Is there a typical life line for your group? If so, what does it look like? Draw it here:

    b. How do life lines differ within the group?

    c. How many of the decisions that have affected your life did you actually make?

    d. What have been the major outside influences on your life? How have these influences changed over time?

    e. Have you learned anything that surprised you?

    f. What do you expect the life lines of members of other groups to look like?

4. Participate in a class discussion based on the above questions, making note of and discussing similarities and differences between groups. (remaining time)

REFERENCE   Carroll, L. (1962). *Alice's adventures in Wonderland.* Middlesex, England: Penguin. (Original work published 1865)

Networking Role Play

Purpose:
1. To demonstrate how people form connections in an informal setting.
2. To identify behaviors that facilitate and inhibit the formation of connections.

Preparation: None

Time: 75 to 90 minutes

INTRODUCTION

Much popular writing has emphasized the value of personal networks in searching for and obtaining desirable jobs and in promoting advancement within organizations. In fact, some organizations promote networking among women professionals to counteract the exclusion of women from "old boy" networks. Women and men with more fully developed organizational networks are likely to see their career success enhanced. However, interactions that take place in informal settings may be just as important in influencing how others see us and what our working relationships with them are like. The purpose of this exercise is to examine how informal networks between people are established.

INSTRUCTIONS

1. The instructor will form 15-person groups in different areas of the classroom with tables and chairs removed or put to the side. Within

AUTHOR'S NOTE: This exercise was prepared by Joyce M. Girard, Cara L. Herman, Gary N. Powell, and Linda M. Salafia.

each group, 13 participants will receive a brief "personality profile" and the other two participants will act as observers and receive a copy of all personality profiles. If you are a role player, familiarize yourself with your role before the role play begins. (15 minutes)

2. In the role play, you have just arrived at a cocktail party being held by an acquaintance in New York City. Feel free to mingle with other guests, whom you are meeting for the first time. (30 minutes)

3. Participate in a class discussion based on the following questions: (remaining time)

    a. What did it feel like to interact with strangers in an informal setting?

    b. Did participants interact freely during the cocktail party?

    c. Were participants eager to help each other when they had the opportunity to do so? Were participants willing to introduce a person in need to an individual who might be able to help him or her?

    d. How strong were the connections established between people by the end of the role play?

    e. What specific behaviors helped or restricted the formation of connections between people?

    f. How do responses to these questions differ between groups?

Dual Careers Role Play

Purpose:	1. To examine problem-solving behavior in decisions concerning dual careers.
	2. To examine decision making in a dyad when each individual's satisfaction with the decision is dependent on the other's satisfaction.
Preparation:	None
Time:	90 minutes

INTRODUCTION More than ever before, women and men are finding themselves taking into account the work career of another person in planning and managing their own work careers. The term *dual-career couple* is not restricted to couples who are married, heterosexual, or even sharing a home; instead, it refers to two people, both of whom work, who are planning their lives together, whether they live together or apart. This planning effort typically requires a high degree of coordination, and frustration may occur when decisions involving trade-offs between the personal interests of the two partners have to be made. The purpose of this exercise is to examine problem-solving behavior when couples have to make difficult decisions regarding dual-career issues.

AUTHOR'S NOTE: This exercise was prepared by Richard B. Carreau, Larry M. Cross, Cynthia B. Dennis, Dolores T. Inkpen, Dorothy H. Mucha, Gary N. Powell, and Kathleen M. Stalk.

INSTRUCTIONS

1. The instructor will form three-person groups. Within each group, one participant will play Partner 1, one will play Partner 2, and the third will act as an observer. Partners 1 and 2 will receive role descriptions, and the observer will receive both role descriptions and a Guidelines for Observers sheet. If you are playing Partner 1 or 2, familiarize yourself with your role before the role play begins. (10 minutes)

2. Conduct the first role play. (15 minutes maximum)

3. The instructor will distribute new role descriptions to Partners 1 and 2 and both role descriptions to the observer. If you are playing Partner 1 or 2, familiarize yourself with the new role description. (10 minutes)

4. Conduct the second role play. (15 minutes maximum)

5. Within your group, discuss the observer's observations. (10 minutes)

6. Participate in a class discussion based on the Guidelines for Observers and the following questions: (remaining time)

    a. What was the range of solutions arrived at by couples?

    b. To what extent were these solutions satisfactory to both members of the couple?

    c. Would you characterize the various couples as

        (1) *Superordinate*—Both partners have the goal of satisfaction in both career and family domains.

        (2) *Synchronized*—The partners have complementary individual goals, with one more interested in family and the other in career.

        (3) *Synthetic*—One or both partners feel that they have compromised their goals.

        (4) *Severed*—The partners have highly incompatible goals.

    d. What behaviors helped couples to reach mutually satisfactory decisions? What behaviors restricted their ability to reach such decisions?

The Mommy Track

Purpose:
1. To identify issues related to "mommy tracks."
2. To increase awareness of employee, employer, and co-worker reactions to the mommy track.

Preparation: Read the Mommy Track Script.

Time: 60 minutes

INTRODUCTION

The increase in the proportion of women managers in recent years has led many organizations to reconsider their assumptions about how managers should deal with family concerns. Through lack of action to the contrary, organizations traditionally have let their employees fend for themselves in satisfying their family needs. Work has been assumed to be a good employee's primary concern, with family issues dealt with and left at home. The model of a successful career has been an uninterrupted sequence of promotions to positions of greater responsibility, heading toward the top ranks. Any request to take time out from or temporarily de-emphasize career for family reasons, by either a woman or a man, has been seen as evidence of lack of career commitment.

Felice Schwartz's (1989) *Harvard Business Review* article, "Management Women and the New Facts of Life," suggested a new posture by organizations in their human resource management policies and practices regarding working women. Although she did not use the term herself, Schwartz triggered a heated debate over the merits of *mommy*

AUTHOR'S NOTE: This exercise was prepared by John W. Franchina, Nancy T. Glass, Sallie W. Howell, Andree R. Kiely, Christine L. LeMoal, Gary N. Powell, and Rosemary T. Smith.

tracks. She proposed that corporations (a) distinguish between "career-primary women" who put their careers first and "career-and-family women" who seek a balance between the two, (b) nurture the careers of the former group as potential top executives, and (c) offer flexible work arrangements and family supports to the latter group in exchange for fewer opportunities for career advancement. Women were assumed to be more interested in such arrangements, and thereby less likely to be suitable top executives, than were men; there has been much less discussion about the merits of "daddy tracks."

Schwartz provoked strong and diverse reactions from many sectors of society. Some felt that her proposal was the answer to an unacknowledged dilemma, both for organizations in making best use of their female talent and for working mothers in striking a desirable balance between work and family. Others saw Schwartz's proposal as a betrayal of decades of progress toward equal status for women in the workplace. Although most commentary in the popular media has focused on the difficulties encountered by the working mother in balancing career and family responsibilities, implementation of mommy track arrangements also creates problems for management and co-workers. The purpose of this exercise is to present, from several perspectives (the immediate supervisor, a senior manager, male and female peers, and the working mother herself), the issues that arise when organizations implement mommy tracks.

INSTRUCTIONS

1. Prior to class, read the Mommy Track Script.

2. Participate in a class discussion based on the following questions:

   a. Scene 1, Employee Request

      (1) What are the pros and cons of the mommy track for the employee?

      (2) How do you feel about the employee's request?

      (3) How do you feel about the employee?

      (4) How far should management go to accommodate an individual's outside interests, even if they don't enhance the company?

      (5) Does the mommy track promote a separate but equal, or unequal, role structure?

(6) Are mommy trackers at risk of losing critical experience and capabilities because of reduced working hours?

b. Scene 2, Management's Reaction

(1) What are the pros and cons of the mommy track for management?

(2) How do you feel about management's granting of the employee's request?

(3) In your own organization (if applicable), how would you and/or management deal with a similar request?

(4) Should management be devoted to fitting women into the existing culture, or finding ways to change that culture?

(5) Are women penalized regardless of their individual career goals and talents, because management sees a danger of their losing commitment to their jobs?

(6) If management is supportive of alternative work arrangements, how can it design and implement an appropriate policy?

(7) How would you make flexible schedules for parents cost-effective?

c. Scene 3, Co-workers' Reactions

(1) What are the pros and cons of the mommy track for co-workers?

(2) What are your reactions to the co-workers' feelings?

(3) How does the mommy track affect workplace morale?

(4) Are mommy trackers less likely to get help and mentoring from superiors and co-workers?

(5) Will co-workers request a reduced schedule in response to the mommy tracker?

d. General Questions

(1) Should organizations make mommy tracks and daddy tracks available to their employees?

(2) If so . . .

(a) How should employees be selected for such arrangements?

(b) How should performance standards differ for employees on the mommy or daddy track versus other employees, if at all?

(c) How should opportunities for advancement and other rewards differ for employees on the mommy or daddy track versus other employees, if at all?

REFERENCE   Schwartz, F. N. (1989, January/February). Management women and the new facts of life. *Harvard Business Review,* pp. 65-76.

THE MOMMY TRACK SCRIPT

CAST

Andree: Department head, who wants a balanced lifestyle and is requesting part-time work.
Rosemary: Vice president, immediate manager of Andree.
Nancy: Executive vice president, immediate manager of Rosemary, who is concerned with trend of women's attrition.
Christine: Co-worker of Andree.
John: Co-worker of Andree.

SCENE 1, EMPLOYEE REQUEST

Setting: Andree, a valued employee, meets with Rosemary, her manager, to request a flexible work schedule to allow her to balance both career and home demands.

Andree: Thank you for setting aside this time for me. I requested the meeting to discuss with you my future role in the organization.

Rosemary: You know we are very happy with you. Your department is one of the best-performing departments in the organization, and your co-workers and subordinates think very highly of you.

Andree: Thank you. I have come to a point in my life where I have to realistically look at myself—where I am and what I want out of life. I have always worked to my fullest, and I have come to realize that the personal cost of my continuing to work full-time is too high. My family and I have discussed my concerns, and I am requesting to continue in my role here, but on a part-time basis. With this flexibility, I can be maximally productive.

Rosemary: I am surprised to hear this. Nancy and I were just discussing your department's excellent performance and the possibilities of a promotion for you. She commented that she was pleased to see that you had made a full commitment to the organization. She said you had shown that we can really rely on you in the long run.

Andree: I know that you take this request as a sign of my decreased motivation and commitment, but I am asking you to see it more as a realistic appraisal of what one person can do.

Rosemary: Go on . . .

Andree: I find that I can no longer "do it all." My children are becoming very active in sports and school activities, and I would like to participate more in their lives. Because of this, I need more balance in my life. I no longer want to put in the hours and weekends that are required of a full-time position. I feel that by reducing my hours I will be less stressed. I will be able to contribute more and perhaps even do more for you because I am not so narrowly focused on my job alone. Can't we explore a flexible solution that would allow me to be productive for the organization and still respond to my family's needs?

Rosemary: You put me in an uncomfortable situation. My responsibility is to get the job done for the organization. You're a valuable manager, but you're putting me in a position where I must produce with a diminished staff.

Andree: I anticipated these concerns. I have a proposal: After a 3-month leave, I would work from 9 a.m. to 3 p.m. Monday through Thursday and be available by phone or fax during the business hours I am away from the office. I request that all my meetings be held between 10 a.m. and 2 p.m. I don't know how my co-workers will react, which concerns me. I will need more of their help and cooperation due to my change in hours.

Rosemary: I am not sure how Nancy will react to your request. I must say I am disappointed, but I can understand your need to have more balance in your life. The one thing we don't want is to lose you or to have you "burn out" trying to do it all. I will present this proposal to Nancy in that light. The big issue will be the impact this will have on the organization as a whole.

Andree: Thank you for understanding. I in no way want to imply that I intend to "slack off" or am less committed to doing my best for the organization. The balance that I need is a result of a realistic appraisal of my life and what I as a person can emotionally and physically do. I always thought I could have it all. Now I realize that, hopefully, I can have it all; I just can't have it all at once.

SCENE 2, MANAGEMENT'S REACTION

Setting: Rosemary meets with Nancy Morgan, an executive vice president and her own manager, to discuss Andree's request for a flexible work schedule.

Rosemary: Andree has just requested a 3-month leave and a flexible work schedule arrangement. It's a shame—I had high hopes for her.

Nancy: She's not the only one in the division who's requested leave. We are losing a lot of good talent! People want a career and a family life.

Rosemary: I can't believe it. I'll have to reschedule the Jones project. It was supposed to start in 6 months. How can I get someone else up to speed in that time?

Nancy: If only we had the vision to plan for people's desire to let career take a back burner occasionally. This organization is a bit old-fashioned in its requirements to give 120% to get ahead and keep ahead. Now we lose good talent like Andree because we don't allow for flexible work schedules or child care considerations.

Rosemary: I've invested a lot of training in Andree. She should be committed to her organization. She should have indicated that her heart wasn't totally into her career. When she worked hard and stayed late over the past 2 years, I figured she was in it for the long haul. I'm really losing a valuable resource!

Nancy: Remember last year when Paul Anderson gave up the bid for junior VP to work at the hunting lodge? I guess everyone has to make choices about the place career has in the big picture of life.

Rosemary: Yes, but Paul is gone for good. Andree wants to come back to work part-time. She even mentioned something as ridiculous as job sharing. When you work for me, you work 70 hours a week. What are the other professionals going to say about Andree? She gets off easy and they pull her weight.

Nancy: Part-time work commands part-time pay and benefits. Perhaps the other employees forget that. Andree's talents aren't less; she just will be spending less time here. You did lighten up the assignments when John Smith was running for mayor—isn't that the same thing? We have to view people's need for balance of career and outside activities equally.

Rosemary: We allow for paternity leave here, but you know the score—anyone who takes it is off the fast track for good. And what about the promotion we have lined Andree up for? We had it all planned that when Steve moved we would put Andree in that job and so on up the ladder. Now I'll have to start grooming someone else for the fast track.

Nancy:	Must we have everyone on the fast track? Having some talented people in the middle-management ranks of this organization may be a good thing. Middle management here is either a dead end or a stepping-stone to the top. We could use some people in those jobs who aren't always focused on getting out of them. Some people think middle management is where the work gets done—having people like Andree there for a few years may really improve the picture of middle management. But I know that if the organization doesn't become more responsive to these needs—by providing child care and flexible work hour alternatives—we can count on losing valuable talent and have little hope of recruiting the best and brightest of tomorrow.
Rosemary:	Why do we need to bend over backward to accommodate the special needs of family-oriented women? Work is for work. If they can't hack it, let them stay home!
Nancy:	In the long run, this organization will need to tap *all* available resources for talent to be more productive. If we recognize the needs of our employees as individuals we can be more competitive in this changing environment.

SCENE 3, CO-WORKERS' REACTIONS

Setting:	After a 3-month leave, Andree returns to work and meets with her peers, Christine and John.
Christine:	Welcome back, Andree!
Andree:	Thanks, Chris. It's good to be back.
John:	How are the kids doing?
Andree:	They're great, John—growing fast.
Christine:	This project is so complex, we're really all going to have to put in lots of extra hours to meet the deadline. It's 3:45, so let's sit down and begin our meeting.
Andree:	Well, I've had a little problem with the software. It's new, and I'm still at the manual stage.
John:	I guess you were on leave when we all took the training course. I kept a notebook with all my notes from the training sessions. If you have any questions on anything in here, let me know. You know how terrible my handwriting is.
Christine:	I suggest we divide the tasks, then each spend tomorrow morning writing. Can we agree to meet at noon tomorrow with rough drafts prepared?
Andree:	Oh, my! (looks at watch) I have to dash off to pick up the baby. I'm sorry—leave whatever you have on my desk and I'll get to it tomorrow. I'm really sorry but I have to leave. (Andree leaves.)
John:	I can't believe that they promoted Andree to account representative like the rest of us after all the time she has taken off.
Christine:	Andree is a talented and hardworking team member, but she's been away for 3 months and she's fallen behind. She needs help.
John:	If she thinks I'm going to hold her hand through all of her assignments, she has another think coming! Does the organization expect us to retrain her and do our own jobs too? I'd like to get on that "mommy track" gimmick. Maybe I'll try to get on the "daddy track." Then my wife and kids might see me home for dinner more often.
Christine:	I put off having kids because I don't want to be on the wrong side of the "glass ceiling." Maybe now management is waking up to the possibilities that not every good performer is cut out to be a workaholic.
John:	And another thing—she had better be making less money than we are or Nancy Morgan will hear about this from me!

Christine: Well, I don't know. She has more experience and her hours are almost full-time. They say she makes and takes calls at home.

John: No one can really work from home. She's sitting and reading the paper or cooking and getting paid for it!

Christine: Well, I do have a lot of questions on how the organization will react to Andree's arrangement, but I'm optimistic. This is a step in the right direction.

26

Becoming a Minority

Purpose:	1. To expose you to cultural differences between yourself and others in a self-chosen environment that is unfamiliar to you.
	2. To increase understanding of how cultural differences influence feelings of comfort and relationships between people in social settings.
Preparation:	Complete the assignment described below.
Time:	90 minutes

INTRODUCTION

The demographic composition of the American labor force is changing, as the proportions of both women and members of minority groups (Hispanic American, Asian American, Native American, and African American and other) have steadily increased in recent years. By the year 2000, the proportion of women in the labor force, which was 42% in 1980 and 45% in 1990, is expected to be 47%; the proportion of minority group members, which was 17% in 1980 and 21% in 1990, is expected to be 25%. White non-Hispanic men, once the majority group in the labor force, will represent only 40%, White non-Hispanic women will constitute 35%, minority men 13%, and minority women 12% (Powell, 1993, p. 226). As a result, organizations whose management practices have been more appropriate for a homogeneous group of

AUTHOR'S NOTE: This exercise was prepared by Renate R. Mai-Dalton. It is reprinted from "Exposing Business School Students to Cultural Diversity: Becoming a Minority" in *Organizational Behavior Teaching Review* (Vol. 9 No. 3, 1984-1985, pp. 76-82). Used with permission.

employees will have to make adjustments to attract and retain talented individuals from diverse groups.

Given these changes, most workers will not be effective at their jobs unless they acquire skills in dealing with culturally different co-workers whom they work with, work for, and supervise. The purpose of this exercise is to give you the opportunity to personally experience cultural differences in an unfamiliar setting.

INSTRUCTIONS

1. The following assignment will expose you to a new situation, require you to observe your surroundings carefully, and ask you to describe both what you felt and what you think other individuals might have felt to have you among them. Your task is to go *by yourself* to a place where you have not been before and observe what you see. To give you some ideas about possible places to visit, here are examples of previous participants' choices:

   a. Protestants visited a Catholic church service and vice versa.

   b. Caucasians visited African American churches.

   c. Participants with sight went to a school for the blind; those with hearing went to a school for the deaf.

   d. A heterosexual participant went to a party for individuals with other sexual preferences.

   e. A "weakling" visited a bodybuilding club.

   f. A younger participant visited a nursing home.

   g. A woman went to a car auction with predominantly male customers.

   There are, of course, many other possibilities. Think of a situation that you have wondered about and want to get to know. Do not choose a setting where you would feel like an intruder into someone's privacy, however, and do not place yourself in a situation that is physically dangerous to you. If in doubt, telephone in advance and inquire if your presence is acceptable to the group. Only choose a setting that you sincerely want to learn about; this will prevent you from feeling like an "undercover agent" and both maintain your integrity and justify your visit.

2. Briefly describe your experience below:

Date and address where the experience took place:

Length of time that you were there:

Brief description of the setting:

Your reaction to the situation in terms of your behavior and feelings:

The reaction of the other individuals toward you:

What this experience teaches you about being different from others in your environment:

How your development might be influenced if you were to live or work in such a setting all your life:

3. In class, the instructor will place you in a discussion group of people who have visited similar settings.

4. As a group, discuss what each of you experienced and identify the following: (45 minutes)

   a. similarities and differences of your experiences

   b. advantages and disadvantages of having these experiences

5. Participate in a class discussion based on the following questions: (remaining time)

   a. What similarities and differences were there between the different settings visited?

   b. What did it feel like to be in the minority?

   c. Did you behave differently from how you normally behave? In what ways?

   d. What are the advantages and disadvantages of putting yourself in a situation where you are in the minority?

   e. How might you behave differently if you were permanently in a minority position, either where you live or work? How might your motivation to work, study, or otherwise achieve be affected?

REFERENCE   Powell, G. N. (1993). *Women and men in management* (2nd ed.). Newbury Park, CA: Sage.

Affirmative Action or Reverse Discrimination?

Purpose:	1. To examine the implications of the legal mandate for American organizations regarding affirmative action. 2. To examine the issue of whether affirmative action necessarily leads to reverse discrimination.
Preparation:	Complete questionnaire.
Time:	90 to 120 minutes

INTRODUCTION

Since the 1960s, American organizations have been under legal pressure to refrain from discrimination and to counteract the effects of past discrimination. Most have been required to take "affirmative action" to promote equal opportunity in employment. By "acting affirmatively," employers go beyond merely refraining from discriminatory practices; they make sure that current decisions and practices enhance the employment, development, and retention of members of protected groups such as women and minorities. Although enforcement of equal opportunity laws has varied from one presidential administration to the next, organizations have learned that violation can be quite costly, both in terms of money and negative public relations.

Title VII of the Civil Rights Act of 1964 and the Equal Pay Act of 1963 are the most significant pieces of federal equal employment opportunity (EEO) legislation. Title VII prohibits discrimination on the basis of sex, race, color, religion, or national origin in any employment condition, including hiring, firing, promotion, transfer, compensation,

AUTHOR'S NOTE: This exercise was inspired by a classroom assignment used by Gary N. Chaison at Clark University.

and admission to training programs. It was later extended to ban discrimination because of pregnancy, childbirth, or related conditions and to ban sexual harassment (see Exercise 14, "Dealing With Sexually Oriented Behavior"). The Equal Pay Act makes it illegal to pay members of one sex at a lower rate than the other if they are in jobs that require equal skill, effort, and responsibility under similar working conditions in the same establishment. Other laws have prohibited discrimination against older people and against qualified people with disabilities (Sedmak & Levin-Epstein, 1991).

Executive Order 11246 prohibits organizations with federal government contracts of more than $10,000 per year from discriminating against any employee or job applicant because of sex, race, religion, color, or national origin. In addition, all organizations with 50 or more employees and federal contracts exceeding $50,000 per year are required to develop written affirmative action plans and to take steps to eliminate discrimination in hiring, firing, layoff, recall, promotion, compensation, working conditions, and facilities. An acceptable affirmative action program must include an analysis of areas in which the organization is underrepresented by women and minority group members as well as specific goals and timetables to remedy any problems.

The whole notion of affirmative action arouses strong emotions in our society. Affirmative action programs that increase the chances that members of one group will be hired, promoted, or paid more are often objected to as "reverse discrimination" by members of other groups. When individuals feel that they or members of their group have been hired because of affirmative action rather than their competence, they may object to the programs as well. The purpose of this exercise is to explore feelings, beliefs, and legal issues regarding whether affirmative action programs necessarily constitute reverse discrimination.

INSTRUCTIONS

1. Prior to class, complete the following questionnaire:

   a. Do affirmative action programs represent a major step toward ensuring equal employment opportunities for all workers?

1	2	3	4	5
definitely disagree	probably disagree	neutral	probably agree	definitely agree

b. Do affirmative action programs represent a major threat to the career progress of workers who do not belong to protected groups?

1	2	3	4	5
definitely disagree	probably disagree	neutral	probably agree	definitely agree

c. When selection and promotion decisions are made by organizations, do protected-group members receive too many breaks?

1	2	3	4	5
definitely disagree	probably disagree	neutral	probably agree	definitely agree

d. Do affirmative action programs necessarily lead to reverse discrimination?

1	2	3	4	5
definitely disagree	probably disagree	neutral	probably agree	definitely agree

Why or why not?

2. In class, the instructor will set up a debate of the question, "Does affirmative action constitute reverse discrimination?" by dividing the class into three groups:

a. "Yes" group: those who would answer yes to the question.

b. "No" group: those who would answer no to the question.

c. "Undecided" group: those who are unsure of their answer to the question.

The debate will be between representatives of the "yes" and "no" groups, with members of the "undecided" group acting as judges.

3. Members of the "yes" and "no" groups should select a representative and help him or her to prepare for the debate. The "undecided" group members should decide the criteria by which the debate will be judged. (20 minutes)

4. *Round 1 of the debate:* The two representatives have 7 minutes each to present their initial arguments, with the order of presentation determined by a coin toss. (15 minutes)

5. Representatives consult with their groups to prepare for rebuttals. (10 minutes)

6. *Round 2 of the debate:* The two representatives rebut each other's arguments. (15 minutes maximum)

7. The judges reach a decision as to which representative, if either, won the debate. (10 minutes maximum)

8. The judges announce their decision and rationale. (5 minutes)

9. Participate in a class discussion of the debate, incorporating responses to the questionnaire where applicable. (remaining time)

REFERENCE   Sedmak, N. J., & Levin-Epstein, M. D. (1991). *Primer on equal employment opportunity* (5th ed.). Washington, DC: Bureau of National Affairs.

28

Goodchips Electronics

Purpose:	1. To examine how affirmative action programs may yield unexpected results.
	2. To identify the characteristics of effective affirmative action programs.
Preparation:	Read the letter from the president of Goodchips Electronics Company.
Time:	4.5 hours over multiple class sessions

INTRODUCTION

To promote equal opportunity, an organization needs a sound management system that analyzes its employment of women and minority group members, identifies problem areas, establishes an action plan based on specific goals and timetables, and then monitors results against the plan. As one executive said in a Conference Board survey:

> How do you go about achieving EEO results in a company? The same way you achieve any other results. You analyze the problem carefully, determine what you need to do, and then set up an overall management planning and control system to make very sure that it happens—and on schedule. (Schaeffer & Lynton, 1979, p. 21)

The purpose of this exercise is to examine how a hypothetical organization chose to adopt an affirmative action program that was ultimately unsuccessful. In so doing, it will shed light on the factors

AUTHOR'S NOTE: This exercise was inspired by a case by S. Lau in *Behavior in Organizations* (rev. ed.). Homewood, IL: Irwin, 1979.

that influence acceptance and effectiveness of affirmative action programs.

INSTRUCTIONS

1. In a prior class, the instructor will have recruited at least four volunteers to play the role of top executives in the Goodchips Electronics Company. The rest of the class will be divided into three management consulting firms with no more than eight participants each. Additional participants will act as observers during the exercise.

2. Your consulting firm (pick a name for yourselves) has received the following letter:

Dear XYZ Consulting Company:

Our company employs over 10,000 people in its nonunionized West Coast plant that makes computer chips. It is located in an area with large proportions of African Americans, Hispanic Americans, and Asian Americans. Its hiring policy for years has been to see that these groups are represented as employees in the same proportions as in the outside population. We have more than succeeded in this, although these groups are not as well represented in managerial ranks.

However, we have been even less successful in moving women into management positions. Six months ago, after discussion with my staff as to the best course of action, we compiled a list of women in the company who were considered most eligible for management positions and offered them promotions accordingly. (Most women are presently in secretarial, clerical, or other support positions, with a few on the factory floor.) Of the 25 women we selected, only 2 of them actually agreed to accept advancement. As for the others, all had one excuse or another for not wanting additional responsibility. Needless to say, this does not really give us a successful program—two women managers out of hundreds of women employees.

By this letter, I am extending to you an invitation to submit a proposal for consulting services to rectify this matter. I am willing to pay you $10,000 for your efforts in preparing a proposal, regardless of whether we accept it. Our expectation is that you will use the billing rate of $1,000/person/day for any further services that you propose.

If you are interested in proceeding, I will make available to you several of my top staff (see partial organization chart below) in addition to myself for interviews. Please call my secretary to set up the necessary appointments. After you have had the opportunity to conduct interviews, we will entertain your proposal. You should know that I am extending this invitation to other consulting companies as well.

I look forward to hearing from you soon.

Best wishes,

Joseph Morgan
President, Goodchips Electronics Company

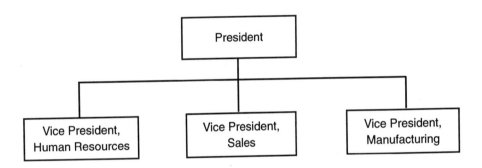

3. In class, the instructor will announce which Goodchips executives will be interviewed by the consulting firms and will make appointments for them. Prepare to interview these executives. (30 minutes)

4. Interviews: (60 minutes in total)

   a. *Round 1:* Your firm will interview _____. (15 minutes)

   b. Break (10 minutes)

   c. *Round 2:* Your firm will interview _____. (15 minutes)

   d. Break (5 minutes)

   e. *Round 3:* Your firm will interview _____. (15 minutes)

5. Consultants should prepare a 10-minute presentation to be delivered to Morgan and the other executives interviewed, using materials provided by the instructor if needed (transparencies, newsprint, marking pens, etc.). Goodchips executives should meet separately to discuss their interviews and impressions of the consulting firms gained so far. (60 minutes)

6. Consultants make their presentations to Morgan and his staff. Each presentation should be made as if other consultants were not present; later presentations should not "borrow" or comment on proposals in earlier ones. Fifteen minutes will be allotted for each presentation to allow time for questions from Goodchips executives. (45 minutes)

7. Goodchips executives hold a staff meeting to decide which consulting firm's proposal, if any, will be accepted. The entire class will silently observe this meeting. (15 minutes maximum)

8. Morgan announces the results of the staff meeting. (5 minutes)

9. Participate in a class discussion based on the following questions: (remaining time)

   a. Regarding the *content* of proposals:

      (1) What do they assume that the real problem is?

      (2) How do they differ in addressing the problem?

      (3) What is the likelihood that the proposed solution will be implemented?

      (4) Is the issue of how the solution would be implemented addressed? If so, is the recommended implementation process appropriate for this company?

   b. Regarding the *development* of proposals:

      (1) How did the interviews go from the consultants' perspectives?

      (2) How did the interviews go from the Goodchips executives' perspectives?

   c. Regarding the *presentation* of proposals:

      (1) Was professionalism demonstrated in the presentation style and emphasis?

(2) Were the consultants responsive to questions by Goodchips staff during the presentation?

d. Regarding the *likely effectiveness* of each proposal:

(1) Does it address the attitudinal barriers to women's advancement that may be present in some Goodchips executives?

(2) Does it address the likely reactions of the targeted group to the program?

(3) Does it stress the importance of a display of commitment and involvement by Morgan in whatever program is adopted?

(4) Does it encourage specification of goals and objectives and appropriate rewards or punishments according to whether goals and objectives are met?

(5) Does it encourage participation of the people affected in the design and implementation of a program?

(6) Does it move away from programs that select women because they are women and emphasize programs that reward talented people instead?

REFERENCE   Schaeffer, R. G., & Lynton, E. F. (1979). *Corporate experiences in improving women's job opportunities*. New York: Conference Board.

Diversity Incidents

Purpose:	1. To help you become more aware of what it means to have a diverse workforce.
	2. To help you formulate ways to deal more effectively with situations in which diversity plays a role.
Preparation:	Read and analyze diversity incidents.
Time:	75 to 90 minutes

INTRODUCTION

Organizations that promote equal opportunity do not necessarily value cultural diversity within their ranks. Equal employment opportunity was originally a legalistic response mandated by the federal government to end discrimination according to sex, race, color, religion, and national origin. Affirmative action programs, which are an outgrowth of equal opportunity law, have contributed to *quantitative* changes in the composition of the workforce in many organizations. In contrast, organizations that value cultural diversity attempt to bring about *qualitative* changes through increased appreciation of the range of skills and values that dissimilar employees offer and increased opportunity to manage work groups that include members who are culturally distinct from the dominant group (Loden & Rosener, 1991, pp. 196-199).

Taylor Cox (1991) distinguished between three types of organizations according to their basic attitudes toward cultural diversity. *Mono-*

AUTHOR'S NOTE: This exercise was prepared by John F. Veiga and John N. Yanouzas. Copyright by John F. Veiga and John N. Yanouzas at the University of Connecticut. Used with permission.

lithic organizations are characterized by a large majority of one group of employees, especially in the managerial ranks. Differences between majority and minority group members are resolved by the process of assimilation, whereby minority group employees are expected to adopt the norms and values of the majority group to survive in the organization. Such organizations are characterized by low levels of intergroup conflict, because there are few members of minority groups and such members have outwardly adopted, if not inwardly embraced, majority norms and values.

Plural organizations have a more heterogeneous workforce than monolithic organizations, primarily because they take steps to be more inclusive of minority group members. These steps may include hiring and promotion policies that stress recruitment and advancement of members of minority groups and manager training on equal opportunity issues. Plural organizations emphasize an affirmative action approach to managing diversity by focusing on the numbers of majority versus minority group members in different jobs and levels, but not on the quality of work relationships between members of different groups. Although the primary organizational approach to resolving cultural differences is assimilation, intergroup conflict can be high if members of the majority group resent practices used to boost minority group membership. Even though overt discrimination may have been banished, prejudice is still likely to exist in plural organizations.

An organization that simply contains many diverse groups of employees is considered a plural organization. *Multicultural organizations* value this diversity. They respond to cultural differences by encouraging members of different groups to adopt some of the norms and values of other groups, in contrast to the assimilation practiced by monolithic and plural organizations. A multicultural approach "involves increasing the consciousness and appreciation of differences associated with the heritage, characteristics, and values of many different groups, as well as respecting the uniqueness of each individual" (Morrison, 1992, p. 7). Intergroup conflict in multicultural organizations is low due to a general absence of prejudice and discrimination.

Thus, to encourage appreciation of diversity among their employees, organizations need to be multicultural in their managerial approach rather than expecting everyone to adhere to the values and norms associated with the traditional majority group. However, what does it really mean to be multicultural and to value differences between employees? The purpose of this exercise is to examine a series of situations, all of which are based on real-life incidents, in which someone feels unfairly treated. In analyzing these situations, you should gain greater appreciation of the wide range of employee differences and kinds of employee treatment that raise questions about how to manage a diverse workforce.

INSTRUCTIONS

1. Prior to class, read the diversity incidents and record your preliminary analysis of each on the analysis page that follows the incidents by responding to the following questions:

   a. Has *discrimination* taken place against an employee who is different from other employees in some way? (If so, is it legally justified?)

   b. Is there *prejudice* against the employee?

   c. Is the employee *oversensitive?*

   d. Has the situation been *managed poorly?*

2. In class, form groups of three to six members.

3. As a group, select one or two incidents to discuss. Codify each incident according to the analysis questions and discuss how the situation could have been handled differently by all parties involved. (30 minutes)

4. The instructor will solicit suggestions from participants for incidents to be discussed by the entire class. (remaining time, allowing about 15 minutes per incident)

REFERENCES

Cox, T., Jr. (1991). The multicultural organization. *Academy of Management Executive, 5*(2), 34-47.

Loden, M., & Rosener, J. B. (1991). *Workforce America! Managing employee diversity as a vital resource.* Homewood, IL: Irwin.

Morrison, A. M. (1992). *The new leaders: Guidelines on leadership diversity in America.* San Francisco: Jossey-Bass.

DIVERSITY INCIDENTS

Because these incidents depict real-life situations, they may cause discomfort to some readers. However, they are not intended to degrade or diminish respect for any racial, ethnic, gender, age, religious, or other groups.

1. Just Getting Old

Background

A large company facing declining profits ordered all managers to reduce costs by 15%. Bob Kelly, a young manager in the accounting office, thought that this was a good opportunity to tighten up on the company's policy of liberal employee benefits and that a good place to begin was in his own unit.

Accounting Manager

Bob Kelly, the youngest person in the accounting office, did not take long to spot areas of fat that could be cut out. He felt that the accounting unit should set an example for others to follow. The ax fell first on Carole Ralston, who turned in a medical bill for a visit to her physician who diagnosed a pain in her right elbow as work-related tendinitis. Carole's immediate supervisor, Jan Jensen, bumped it up to Bob, who responded a month later by refusing the claim and instructed Jan to tell Carole that she's "just getting old."

Accountant

Carole Ralston was appalled by the treatment she got from the firm. After 16 years of service, she felt betrayed when Bob Kelly rejected a medical bill for a work-related injury and had the audacity to pass it off as "just getting old." Moreover, Carole felt the delay in getting even this negative answer indicated that management had not handled this matter expeditiously. Angered by this treatment, Carole told Jan to tell Bob that it looks like he just doesn't give a damn.

2. That Fat Slob

Background

The Service Department of Computer Universe maintained the computers of many small and large businesses in the area. The large clients who provided lucrative contracts were given extra special attention and service. One such client demanded a change in the specialist who serviced its computers.

Computer Service Manager

Fran Stone, the Computer Service Manager, was dumbfounded when a large client demanded that John Zurn be removed from the account. When Fran asked why, the client claimed that John was incompetent. When the client could not elaborate on the incompetence allegation, the true reason emerged. Pushed to the wall, the client said: "That fat slob couldn't service my chair." To avoid the loss of this account, Fran assigned another service specialist to replace John.

Computer Service Specialist

John Zurn took great pride in his work and was pleased with the list of prestigious clients he worked for. He enjoyed his work and got along fine with everyone but was constantly uneasy about his weight. At 5 ft, 8 in, his weight of 350 pounds was out of control. To help himself bear this cross, John joined the National Association to Advance Fat Acceptance. He is now convinced more than ever that fat people can be excellent at whatever they do. Fran's decision to remove John from this prestigious account is a serious setback for John's newfound confidence.

3. A Pregnant Branch Manager?

Background

A medium-sized bank with 27 branch offices is experiencing high turnover among tellers and managers, especially assistant branch managers. The bank has embarked on a plan to reduce this turnover. In its efforts to engage in strong affirmative action, the bank promoted many females to positions in branch management. Unfortunately, some of these newly promoted managers have left the bank for numerous reasons, one of the main causes being maternity separations.

Vice President of Branch Operations

The VP of branch operations is having some second thoughts about promoting females into branch management positions unless it seems probable that they will not take maternity leave soon. Cora Williams, the branch manager at the Hilltop Branch, has recommended promoting Brenda Stark from head teller to assistant branch manager at Hilltop. The VP is reluctant to do this because Brenda is pregnant and due to take maternity leave in 4 months. The position of coordinator of teller training, a "mommy track" position, would be more appropriate for Brenda, who is good at training tellers.

Branch Manager

Since the assistant branch manager left 3 weeks ago, Cora Williams has been doing the work of two people. She is anxious to fill the position and believes Brenda Stark would be ideal because she is qualified and has a long-term interest in being employed by the bank. Brenda plans to use about half of her maternity leave and then return to work. Failure to promote Brenda to this position would be clearly contrary to the bank's affirmative action program.

4. When Is a "Good Morning" Good?

Background

In recent years, university campuses have experienced some of the problems afflicting society in general concerning ethnic and racial bias and harassment. Students, faculty, administrators, and support staff have been accused of ethnic/racial discrimination, causing numerous universities to adopt numerous antiharassment policies and programs for students as well as faculty aimed at improving racial harmony. But the very effort of trying to define harassment and discrimination on a lively college campus has generated allegations of harassment. A faculty member who was discussing how difficult it is to recognize the subtleties of discrimination and harassment described the following incident that had occurred to a manager:

> A manager greeted the office staff with a "Good morning, it is such a nice day." A Black employee reacted by saying, "It may be a nice day for you but it isn't for my mother who is freezing in her house in Alabama because she cannot afford to buy heating fuel."

The instructor ended the discussion by saying: "Harassment is a subjective matter and we must learn how to define it better." At the end of the instructor's comments, one student left the classroom and returned 15 minutes later. After the session, the student visited the instructor in his office and accused him of engaging in racial discrimination because the incident "made all Blacks look bad."

Instructor

In an effort to make learning more meaningful, the instructor of a course in organizational behavior used experiential methods in the classroom, including exercises, role plays, and discussions. Dealing openly with biases and harassment in organizations was clearly integral to the course and discussing it in class was appropriate and legitimate. Ignoring the race of someone in an incident would mask a crucial fact and would not provide relevant information that students needed to confront racial issues and discuss them.

Student

The student came to the university because she hoped to live in an environment free of racial discrimination, in contrast to the place she came from. The student felt her request to the instructor to refrain from making African Americans look bad was reasonable. She felt that the instructor was presenting a good course but could do it without demeaning any racial group or offending any student. When the instructor did not yield to her request, she became visibly upset and left the office in disgust.

5. The Switchboard

Background

The office manager of a large law firm, the Omega Group, reassigned the visibly pregnant receptionist to be the switchboard operator. The switchboard operator took over at the reception desk.

Office Manager

Several partners of Omega had asked the office manager to remove the receptionist temporarily from the front desk, but he did nothing until a senior partner made the same request. Because the office manager did not really want to make this reassignment, he drafted a memo to the receptionist informing her that this reassignment was only temporary. His hope was that the receptionist would not connect her pregnancy to the reassignment.

Receptionist

The receptionist was somewhat confused by the memo because it did not explain why the reassignment was made. Knowing that the switchboard operator did not enjoy the face-to-face contact with clients made this even more perplexing. Surely, she thought, a group of lawyers would not run the risk of charges of discrimination by making her pregnancy the cause for the reassignment.

6. The Convicted Felon

Background

The Maxx Candy Co. was experiencing a severe shortage of accountants and was urgently trying to fill at least two of its three vacant positions in accounting.

Personnel Manager

The personnel manager placed ads in all of the appropriate places and received only five applications. The best application was from Betty Whitney; however, she had served a short jail sentence for selling narcotics. She had an excellent school record and had done a semester's internship in a corporation similar to Maxx. The personnel manager was somewhat surprised and perplexed when the accounting manager discretely removed Whitney's application.

Accounting Manager

The accounting manager realized that the shortage of accountants in the entire region would complicate and lengthen the search, so he pressed the personnel manager hard to get a search mounted. Quarterly reports were due in 5 weeks, and accounting needed as many hands as possible. The accounting manager was impressed with Betty Whitney's credentials until he came to the information on her criminal conviction. Because Maxx is a candy company that sells a product used by children, he could not hire a convicted felon. Besides, he thought, she would never fit in with the rest of the staff.

7. Reluctant to Be Promoted

Background

Searching to find promotable employees is no less a problem on the production floor than it is in the executive suite. RPW pursues a policy of promoting those who perform well. However, Sam Terry, an assembly worker who is an excellent performer, has refused a promotion offered by his supervisor.

Supervisor

The best assembly worker is Sam Terry, who has worked for RPW for 2 years since graduating from high school. He recently refused a promotion from an entry-level position in the assembly department to the shipping department. Kathy Norman, the supervisor, is really puzzled by this refusal because the promotion would have included a 20% pay increase. She wonders what has happened to upward mobility and the work ethic.

Assembly Worker

Sam Terry was happy working for Kathy Norman at RPW as an assembly worker. Because Sam is functionally illiterate, he appreciated Kathy's permission to take the process manual home on weekends. That way his younger brother or his girlfriend would read it, and then Sam would memorize the steps in each assembly job. With diagrams to remind him, it was easy for Sam to do the assembly work. The job in the shipping department would require Sam to fill parts orders and to read and write. However, Sam could manage no more than his name, address, and phone number.

8. No Habla Español, Aqui

Background

Food Service, Inc., distributes precooked food to 30 locations in a large city. The workforce and clientele consist of over 90% African Americans and Hispanic Americans. Some of the correspondence and advertisements must be done in both English and Spanish. Until recently, the food manager hired professional translators to do this work but now is relying on Anna Maria Luz, a bilingual account clerk, to translate letters and fliers.

Food Manager

Jane Lessard has been the food manager for 20 years and seems to manage effectively though strictly. One of her rules is "English only in the workplace." Troubled by Anna Maria, who frequently converses in Spanish with other employees, the food manager told her to stop violating the English-only rule. Jane believes that Hispanics should be forced to learn the language of their adopted land. After all, she thinks, this is a one-language country. Anna Maria's reaction was to go into a slowdown with Jane's requests for translation work.

Account Clerk

Even though it was not in her job description, doing the translation work did not bother Anna Maria until Jane clamped down on the English-only rule. Because Jane expected Anna Maria to engage in Spanish translations, she felt that Jane should not require her to abide by the English-only rule. Furthermore, Anna Maria felt that some of the Hispanics could do better work if instructions were in Spanish.

9. The Medical Condition

Background

Bill Morrow, the manager of the Underwriting Unit at High Risk Drivers Insurance Co., terminated Pete Nicholson, manager of the Automobile Assigned Risk Unit, who was not performing his duties adequately. Pete had a long and distinguished record with the company, but his performance has slipped ever since he was transferred into Bill's unit. Pete was approving virtually all marginal business and delaying difficult cases that called for underwriter action.

Manager of Underwriting Unit

Ever since Pete was transferred into Bill's unit, his performance has declined. The transfer was done to give Pete a less stressful job after he went through brain surgery for removal of a tumor. Pete's below-average work was tolerated during his postsurgery radiation and chemotherapy period, but now it was time for Pete to come up to average or take disability leave, which provided good medical and income benefits.

Manager of Automobile Assigned Risk Unit

Pete felt that he could handle the less stressful job sufficiently, though not at the same level as before his surgery. He wanted to keep working to give his wife a chance to stay home with their two children. Pete felt he was performing adequately and that Bill was unduly influenced by his knowledge of Pete's medical condition. Moreover, it seemed that Bill's knowledge of Pete's outstanding work in the past was an unfair comparison to apply to the current job requirements.

10. Toenails in the Corner

Background

Dr. Harvey Bernstein owns and operates a private practice in podiatry that employs a receptionist, a female licensed practical nurse (LPN), an orthotic technician, and a janitor. Besides providing the typical services, such as surgery on bunions and bone spurs, foot care, and grooming, Dr. Bernstein constructs orthotic appliances worn in shoes. Florence Walsh, the LPN, has worked 8 years in the office, and her duties include assisting in surgical procedures, preparing examination rooms and equipment, operating the whirlpool, prepping patients for treatment, taping and bandaging, cutting toenails, dispensing instructions, and providing sympathy.

The Doctor

Dr. Bernstein is somewhat concerned about the way Nurse Walsh perceives her duties. It seems that any time the doctor asks her to do any cleanup work she frowns and mutters disapprovingly. She is especially sensitive to the doctor's requests to gather up toenails. Instead of picking them up, she sweeps them into a corner for the janitor to gather after office hours. This irritates the doctor, who thinks picking up toenails is part of Nurse Walsh's cleanup duties.

The Nurse

Nurse Walsh does not object to doing cleanup work but feels that Dr. Bernstein's attitude about gathering up toenails borders on male chauvinism. The doctor gives her the impression that cleanup work is part of "women's work." She believes that nurses are every bit as professional as doctors.

11. Why Me?

Background

The Chase Memorial Hospital, a progressive 1,000-bed teaching facility, has introduced a clinical ladder and merit system to provide an orderly way for nurses to be promoted based on merit. For instance, to be promoted to Clinical II Registered Nurse (RN), one must do a self-evaluation and complete a research project or implement a program appropriate to the needs of patients. To help newly hired nurses prepare themselves for promotion, each one is assigned to a mentor, frequently a nurse with more than 2 years' experience. The clinical ladder and merit system makes it easier to recruit new nurses and retain existing personnel. Assigning mentors to new nurses is decided by the head nurse of a unit.

Head Nurse

Anne Capp, RN, head nurse of a 27-bed oncology unit, is a graduate from the outdated Chase School of Nursing diploma program but is currently working part time on a BS. Although she's a traditionalist, Anne's technical skills and bedside manner are up-to-date. Because the oncology unit is staffed by young, well-trained, and ambitious people, the head nurse maintains a proper distance from the staff but believes she is fair and accessible. Understanding young people, however, is the most difficult part of her job. For instance, she cannot understand why an African American nurse, Esther Wilson, balked at becoming the mentor for a newly hired African American nurse.

Nurse

Esther Wilson has made good progress in her 2 years at Chase, but she has fallen a little behind in preparing her proposal for a special interest program—developing a network of providers for family-centered home care of cancer patients. For 2 years, Anne treated her like a competent nurse, but now Esther feels she is being singled out as an African American nurse. Assigning her to be mentor to a newly hired African American nurse was done without even consulting her. Esther was reluctant to decline the assignment, but it has slowed up her progress. This will delay her eligibility to become Clinical II RN.

12. Skinny Is Beautiful

Background

Diane Nolan, a producer at Primex Investment Corp., is troubled by the reaction of her sales assistant, Georgia Elias. Diane is mentoring Georgia and encouraging her not to be defensive about being skinny. Georgia seems to resent intended ego-boosting comments such as, "You are lucky to be so skinny," "skinny is beautiful," and "skinny people are wiry but tough."

Producer

By her well-meaning comments, Diane is trying to avoid making mistakes that so many others make in relating to skinny people. Her former boss never expressed to Diane any compliment about her work or appearance. As a small girl, Diane, too, was skinny, but her mother taught her that skinny is good and beautiful. Diane is attempting to make Georgia feel better about herself but seems to have run into a stone wall.

Sales Assistant

Georgia Elias does not like being skinny and resents others who make comments about it. To Georgia, skinny means something negative, unhealthy, and ugly. Her mother was skinny when she died of cancer. Many times Georgia has tried to gain weight without any success. Georgia cannot understand why Diane makes so much fuss over skinniness given that she is skinny herself.

13. Nose Tweaking

Background

The engineering department of a medium-sized, consumer-based manufacturing company recently hired its first female engineer, Louise Jameson, who recently graduated with honors from a small college and is currently working on an MBA.

Manager of Engineering

Jim Jacobson has been manager of engineering for 10 years and has developed good rapport with the all-male department. Hiring a female means that he must not only develop a new relationship with her but also monitor how others in the company relate to her. Jim thinks that Louise is doing well in her work and has heard no complaints from others. She is holding her own among the engineers as well as with those she must deal with in technical support units.

Engineer

Louise Jameson thinks she is doing well on her job and was rated above average on her last performance review. Yet she is concerned about how others, especially those in management, perceive her—namely, as very young. She often gets casual comments about her youthfulness and wonders if they reflect doubts about her competence due to her lack of experience and maturity. A more worrisome matter involves the behavior of Jack from shipping, who calls her "Sweetheart" and occasionally tweaks her nose. When he does this, particularly in the presence of others, it is embarrassing and belittling. Louise is in a dilemma about mentioning this to her boss.

14. All Work and No Play

Background

A group of newly hired accountants has just completed the introductory training program in the Audit Department of Peat, Ernst and Anderson in New York City. The assignment of the new auditors to specific clients is done by the audit managers. Matching up auditors to managers and clients is never done to the satisfaction of all parties. Darren Young, one of the newly trained auditors, has complained that he was not assigned any of the clients he had hoped to get and suspects that one of the audit managers, Hank Roberts, is biased in selecting a female to work for him and many of the clients Darren wanted.

Audit Manager

Hank Roberts had an opportunity to survey the new auditors when he was the instructor for 3 days during their training session. He hit it off really well with Cathy Terio because she was a good auditor and also liked to party after class. Hank believes that, with so many young, single people in the profession, one of the perks for working in New York City is the many opportunities to combine work with fun. Otherwise, why put up with all of the stresses of working in New York City?

Auditor

Darren is a bright, pleasant, reserved, and ambitious young accountant who deliberately elected to work in New York after he graduated from a Mormon university in Utah. He wanted to work with the "best and brightest" colleagues and for a wide array of impressive clients. When he learned that

Cathy Terio got the assignments he wanted, Darren reasoned that nonwork criteria, such as partying, having fun, and drinking after work, were more important than his sound qualifications and work ethic. Why should lifestyle enter into assignment decisions?

15. The "Top Five" Club

Background

Kidwell Investments, Inc., a large brokerage house, recently moved into the most prestigious office building in Hartford. To take advantage of the publicity associated with the building, Kidwell ran a full-page promotional ad in the Hartford Daily. It showed the five top brokers (in terms of sales production) in the Hartford office sitting around a U-shaped table, with related copy emphasizing stability, reliability, and dedication. The ad had an immediate impact in terms of increased sales for the brokers pictured. However, it also caused some grumbling, particularly from brokers who did not benefit directly. Rebecca Moore, a high-producing broker, was especially upset.

Vice President

Frank Casey, resident vice president, personally handled the promotional ad and selected the top five brokers because he felt that they presented an image of dependable, high-quality financial service. Frank thought that no matter how many people were selected to be in the ad, others who were not pictured would complain.

Broker

Rebecca Moore made rapid progress in Kidwell and had the sixth best sales record in the office. Her clients include both male and female investors. In her eyes, the old myth about women not being good money handlers was dying fast. To her, the ad looked as if it was a picture taken in a men's-only club. She feels that Frank deliberately selected the top five to keep a female face out of the ad.

16. The White "Minority"

Background

Steve West is supervisor of the Electrical Control Department at APEX, Inc., a manufacturing firm located in New York City. Besides the supervisor, there are four others in the department: Allen Randall, a senior electrical engineer who is a Caucasian American with a BS and an MS in electrical engineering; Da Yu, a junior electrical engineer from China; Jose Rodriguez, a senior technician from Puerto Rico; and Mary Krasinski, an electrical technician from Poland. The crew has worked well together.

Supervisor

Steve West has worked for APEX since coming to the United States from Jamaica 12 years ago. By going to night school, he earned a BS and an MS degree in electrical engineering. Since his being promoted into a supervisory position, doing both engineering design work and management has been a heavy load for him. Hiring Allen seemed like a good way to balance his responsibilities by giving Allen most of the design work. This shift has not worked out well, however, because Steve enjoys doing electrical design and has started to do more of it as new orders come in.

Senior Electrical Engineer

Allen was hired to handle the growing amount of business and to relieve Steve of the overload in electrical design work, but now Steve is taking away some of Allen's design work. Allen thinks Steve may feel threatened by the good design work that he has done and is protecting his position. Allen perceives this as reverse racial discrimination against the lone White male American in the department.

17. Fear of Litigation

Background

Sterling Software, which designs, manufactures, and markets computer systems worldwide, is going through a transition period from 5 years of fast growth to a maturing market.

Branch Manager

Larry Barber is the manager of a branch that employs 20 people, most of whom (13 males and 1 female) are salespeople. The most troublesome employee is Marsha Davies, who 10 years ago showed much promise that has never been realized. Five years ago when Larry was promoted to manager, a dispute arose between Marsha and Don Spaziano over who should get an important account. Larry decided in favor of Don but was forced to reverse his decision at his manager's insistence to avoid a sex discrimination lawsuit that Marsha threatened to initiate. Larry faced a similar dilemma last week. Marsha wants a new and lucrative account and so does John Douglas, who is an above-average salesman. Marsha's sales record is far below her targeted levels. Numerous customer complaints have been received about her, and she has a high absenteeism record. Nonetheless, Larry decided to give the account to Marsha.

Sales Representative

John Douglas, a sales representative, has done well, hitting or surpassing his sales target in every period during his 4 years at Sterling. He feels that Marsha's threat of another sex discrimination suit is being used as an excuse by Larry, who seems to be a spineless manager. John is seriously considering leaving the firm.

18. The "Red-Bone" Incident

Background

The preprocessing unit of the Atlanta Office of the Internal Revenue Service supervised by Ruby Lewis is composed of 14 people, mostly African American females. The average length of service is 8 years, with the shortest time being 9 months. The office ran smoothly until recently when one of the clerks, Tracy Morrow, filed suit in federal court alleging that her discharge was based on racial discrimination. This story attracted national coverage by the news media.

Supervisor

Starting as a clerk typist 10 years ago, Ruby Lewis worked her way up to supervisor and is attending college in the evenings, working on a BS degree in accounting. Most of the women look up to Ruby, and they are encouraged to work hard to advance in the organization. The recent flare-up between Tracy Morrow and three workers in the unit placed Ruby in a difficult position. Tracy, who is a light-skinned Black, claimed that Ruby and others engaged in racial discrimination. When Ruby started monitoring Tracy's work more closely, she found that Tracy was lazy, incompetent, and frequently tardy, and had a negative attitude toward work and her co-workers. Yet Tracy expected to be treated as an equal. This reminded Ruby of stories her grandfather told her about the special favors light-skinned slaves received from the landowners who fathered them. After two official warnings, Ruby discharged Tracy.

Clerical Worker

Tracy came to the Atlanta Office from Seattle but found that work in this office was much more demanding than it was in Seattle. She felt shunned by co-workers who often called her a "red bone" and a "bright," demeaning terms that single out light-skinned Blacks as offspring of mixed-race parents. Ruby began supervising Tracy more closely but did nothing about this harassment. Tracy feels that this close supervision itself was discriminatory because the others were not watched as closely. In Tracy's eyes, this violated equal employment opportunity principles.

19. Siesta Time

Background

An American firm operating a bakery on the U.S. side of the "maquiladora" zone is experiencing difficulties applying U.S. work standards and management practices to Mexicans who come across the border daily to work. Edward Tippett, an American foreman in the truck maintenance and repair shop, is regularly bothered by incidents that he feels would never happen with American workers. All of the employees except Tippett are Mexican. The most troublesome mechanic is Ramon Ramos.

Foreman

Edward Tippett supervises eight mechanics, most of whom are good workers, but Ramon Ramos makes up for the others. He is good but careless, ignores basic safety rules, and insists on making up his own schedule. Often, Ramon eats his lunch during work hours and then takes a siesta during the 20-minute lunch break, except the siesta sometimes lasts for 30 or 40 minutes. This disrupts teamwork and is a violation of the work rules. Ed sees this as part of a casual work attitude that Mexicans bring with them when they cross the border. He believes that Americans did not get ahead by sleeping away the afternoons.

Mechanic

Ramon Ramos is a good mechanic who drives across the border daily to earn twice as much as he would in Mexico. He likes his work, even though at times some of the American expectations on work habits go against all that is Mexican. For instance, the siesta is something that all Mexicans observe. However, when they cross the border, the Americans demand that these cultural mores be left behind. The Americans like to hire Mexicans, pay them far less than they would pay locals, and then expect the Mexicans to behave like Americans. Anyway, Ramos feels he works extra hard and makes up during work time the extra 10 minutes that he spends on his siesta.

20. Lying Down on the Job

Background

An assistant professor of management in her third year of an initial 3-year appointment was reappointed for another 3 years. However, the university's personnel committee, consisting of elected faculty from different disciplines, wrote in her letter of reappointment that she needed to work on improving her teaching performance. The same committee will decide whether or not to grant her tenure during the last year of her second 3-year appointment.

Assistant Professor

Jane Mangalo was extremely angered by the negative reference to her teaching performance in the letter of reappointment. She had received excellent ratings from students in all but one semester. During that semester, she was pregnant and suffered back pain that made it impossible for her to stand or sit for extended periods of time. The pregnancy prevented her from taking pain-relieving medication. In addition, she was forced to teach while lying on her side on a bench in front of the classroom. This prevented her from writing on the blackboard, her usual practice, as she led case discussions. The back problem went away after she had the baby. However, apparently, some students complained about how she taught the class that semester. Jane believed that she did the university a favor by teaching rather than going on disability leave and that the negative reference to her teaching performance in the letter of reappointment constituted discrimination against the disabled.

University Personnel Committee

When the committee found evidence of weak teaching performance by Jane in some of her courses, it decided to include in the letter the standard phrase used in such cases, encouraging her to work on improving her teaching performance, while still reappointing her for another 3 years. When it wrote the letter, the committee was unaware of Jane's condition during the sole semester in which the evidence of weak teaching performance appeared. Although Jane's temporary medical problem was mentioned in the portfolio of materials that the committee reviewed, the reference to it was overlooked.

DIVERSITY INCIDENTS ANALYSIS

INSTRUCTIONS: Respond "yes" or "no" for each incident.

Incident	Discrimination (legally justified?)	Prejudice?	Oversensitivity?	Managed Poorly?
1. Just Getting Old				
2. That Fat Slob				
3. A Pregnant Branch Manager?				
4. When Is a "Good Morning" Good?				
5. The Switchboard				
6. The Convicted Felon				
7. Reluctant to Be Promoted				
8. No Habla Español, Aqui				
9. The Medical Condition				
10. Toenails in the Corner				
11. Why Me?				
12. Skinny Is Beautiful				
13. Nose Tweaking				
14. All Work and No Play				
15. The "Top Five" Club				
16. The White "Minority"				
17. Fear of Litigation				
18. The "Red-Bone" Incident				
19. Siesta Time				
20. Lying Down on the Job				

Developing Diversity Plans Within Diverse Organizations

Purpose:	1. To apply knowledge gained about how to establish an organizational culture that values diversity among its employees (i.e., how to become a multicultural organization).
	2. To identify general principles for how to design and implement a diversity plan.
	3. To examine the internal dynamics that occur when an organization attempts to design and implement a diversity plan.
Preparation:	None
Time:	90 to 120 minutes

INTRODUCTION Organizations are increasingly recognizing that they need to understand and prepare for the changing demographic trends in the labor force. However, different organizations have different diversity-related issues to address. This is partly due to their different demographic profiles but also to their different sizes, histories, industries, and competitive situations. The purpose of this exercise is to examine (a) the process by which organizations develop diversity plans and (b) the content of diversity plans as they relate to differing organizational contexts.

AUTHOR'S NOTE: This exercise was prepared by Judith A. Neal.

INSTRUCTIONS

1. The instructor will form four groups of equal size and assign each group to act as the Diversity Planning Committee for one of the four organizations depicted in the Organizational Profiles. In addition, each group will receive a set of role descriptions for one human resource manager, one White male executive, one White male middle manager, and several nontraditional employees. Each member of the group who is a nontraditional employee will decide which aspect of diversity to represent, which may or may not be one of the groups described in the organizational profile; however, each group described in the profile must be represented. For a more powerful learning experience, take a role that is different from your own racial/ethnic group and/or gender if possible. Familiarize yourself with your role before the group meeting begins. (10 minutes)

2. As a group, prepare a diversity plan for your organization, using the Possible Elements of a Diversity Process as a guide. Prepare a 5-minute presentation to be delivered to the class regarding your diversity plan and rationale for it. (40 minutes)

3. Each group makes its presentation. (20 minutes)

4. Participate in a class discussion based on the following questions: (remaining time)

   a. What are the similarities and differences between the organizational situations?

   b. What are the similarities and differences between the different diversity plans?

   c. How well does each plan respond to the unique situation in which it would be implemented? How could it be improved?

   d. How much attention should be paid to the composition of a Diversity Planning Committee?

   e. What steps can be taken to ensure that the members of a Diversity Planning Committee work well together?

   f. Based on your experiences with this exercise and elsewhere, is there anything in the description of the Possible Elements of a Diversity Process that you would add, delete, change, emphasize, or de-emphasize?

DEVELOPING DIVERSITY PLANS WITHIN DIVERSE ORGANIZATIONS
ORGANIZATIONAL PROFILES

1. *COVENTRY BASKET COMPANY*

This company was founded by Lucille Bowen as a cottage industry in 1938. She began by making baskets as gifts for her friends and as items for church craft sales, and they became so popular that people started ordering them from her on a regular basis. As the orders grew, Lucille taught her daughters the art of weaving baskets, and she moved into a marketing and administrative position. The business continued to grow and is now a regional business in the New England area.

Coventry Basket has remained in the family and is now managed by CEO David Clarke, who is Lucille's grandson. The company headquarters, warehouse, and packaging plant are housed in the small New England town where Lucille started the business in her home. Baskets are now imported from all over the world, although there is still a line of custom-designed baskets that are made by people working out of their homes. However, the major product line is packaging specialty baskets with items such as soaps and candles, gifts for infants, gifts for brides-to-be, and holiday gifts. Not only are baskets distributed to gift shops throughout New England, but the company has just gotten into the mail order business and intends to expand nationally.

The company employs about 300 people. Eighty percent are women and 10% are racial minorities. There is a wide range in ages, although most of the women are between the ages of 20 and 45. All managers, except the human resource manager (a White woman), are White males. Although turnover is low, there is some dissatisfaction in the workforce with career advancement issues and with issues related to parenting.

2. *STATE DEPARTMENT OF HEALTH AND WELFARE*

This state agency is responsible for all statewide programs dealing with health issues as well as the state's welfare program. Some of the agency's duties are monitoring hospitals and other medical facilities to ensure that they are complying with state regulations, monitoring insurance company practices, overseeing immunization programs, and developing plans to educate and train those who are currently on welfare so that they can become self-supporting.

The agency is headed by Daniel Lonhart, a 45-year-old African American with an MBA from a prestigious university. It employs about 750 people and, because of strong affirmative action policies, has a great deal of diversity among employees. The agency's affirmative action plan shows that the demographics of its employee population are well matched to the population of the Midwest U.S. state in which it is located.

Recently, a group of young African Americans asked for a meeting with Lonhart to discuss some problems they were experiencing. They felt that the environment at the agency was hostile to racial minorities, and several reported experiencing name-calling, racial jokes, and even minor damage to cars that they suspect is racially motivated. People of African descent make up the largest racial minority in the agency. The few Hispanics have tended to be promoted faster than members of other minority groups, and the three Asian Americans are in well-paying information systems positions.

The Native Americans are employed almost entirely at the lowest levels of the agency, typically in clerical, janitorial, or driver positions. They have made no complaints of discrimination, but there is unusually high turnover. In general, Native Americans do not like to draw attention to themselves.

In the last 5 years, there have been three lawsuits against the agency claiming discrimination and wrongful discharge. Each of these cases was related to downsizing activities due to budget cutbacks.

3. FREEMAN PHARMACEUTICALS

A large, global corporation based in the United States, this company develops, produces, and markets pharmaceutical products all over the world. Founded in the late 1940s, it has grown dramatically because of its continued investment in R&D and its ability to bring new drugs to market in a timely manner.

As in most corporations of its size—it employs about 50,000 people worldwide—its top managers are mostly White males. However, there is a fair degree of international diversity in top management, because of Freeman's commitment to integrating all of its businesses around the world.

Two years ago, the corporation made a major purchase of a pharmaceutical company in Germany as part of its strategic plan. A number of the German managers were brought to the United States so that they could learn about American business practices and become familiar with Freeman's policies and procedures. Freeman also sent several American managers to the German company so that they could learn some of the new technology recently implemented there as well as learn about German management practices and the European market.

In each case, the relocating managers were supposed to spend a minimum of 18 months in the new country. However, statistics show that the average length of assignment is about 7 months, with both German and American managers making requests to return early to their home countries. This relocation is very expensive, and the president is feeling frustrated about the slow progress of integrating the new acquisition into the Freeman culture.

4. WIZARD CLOTHING

This California-based company designs and distributes clothing for teens and young adults that appeals to rock musicians, artists, actors, concert goers, and those involved in fantasy role-playing games. Wizard Clothing is known for its unique and creative designs, and it has a reputation for being a trendsetter in a demanding and very competitive market.

The company was founded by two hippies in the 1960s who were very involved in the Haight-Ashbury scene in San Francisco. The founders are still in charge and have maintained much of the idealism of the 1960s. As a result, most company policies and practices tend to be very liberal. For example, when Wizard was small, many employees brought their children with them to work. As the company grew, it became natural to create a cooperative, on-site day care center. There is an "anything goes" dress code, except that suits and ties are forbidden. The company has also instituted flextime and job sharing and has a generous tuition reimbursement program.

The workforce (about 2,000 employees) is quite diverse, with no one group being a clear majority, which is representative of California demographics. Many of those who sew the clothing are recent immigrants, and 13 different languages are spoken in the company. Many of the immigrants have trouble speaking and understanding English. In addition, about 20% of the workforce is gay or lesbian, and some of them are asking why the company does not offer the same benefits for them and their partners as those offered to heterosexuals. Also, there is a strong feminist support group that meets after hours (with the company's blessing), and they believe that there is a "glass ceiling" at Wizard. They would like to see changes made that would help women advance further in upper management.

DEVELOPING DIVERSITY PLANS WITHIN DIVERSE ORGANIZATIONS
POSSIBLE ELEMENTS OF A DIVERSITY PROCESS

1. Assess the organization—diagnose diversity issues.

    a. methods

        (1) questionnaire

        (2) interviews

        (3) focus groups

    b. process

        (1) team approach

        (2) outside consultants

2. Gain top management commitment.

    a. position diversity as a key business issue

    b. educate top management

3. Select strategies that meet organizational goals.

    a. training

        (1) separate programs for women and minorities?

        (2) awareness training

        (3) general skills for all managers

    b. measurement beyond affirmative action—focus on business needs

    c. selection processes

    d. career development

    e. performance appraisal and reward systems

    f. evaluate compensation plan and compensation distribution

    g. provide exposure for nontraditional employees

4. Set realistic and measurable short-term and long-term goals.

5. Implement an ongoing process for evaluating diversity issues in the future.

31

Cultural Diversity Consultants

Purpose:
1. To apply knowledge gained about how to establish an organizational culture that values diversity among its employees (i.e., how to become a multicultural organization).
2. To examine the process by which consulting firms assist organizations in their design and implementation of a diversity plan.
3. To identify the conditions under which organizations benefit from using an outside consultant to facilitate the diversity process.

Preparation: None

Time: 2.5 to 3 hours over one or two class sessions

INTRODUCTION

The last exercise, "Developing Diversity Plans Within Diverse Organizations," focused on the internal dynamics that might occur in different types of organizations as they attempt to move from a *monolithic* or *plural* organizational culture to a *multicultural* one (see Exercise 29, "Diversity Incidents," for definitions of these terms). This exercise focuses on the involvement of consultants in the development of diversity plans. It asks you to act as a member of a consulting firm by selecting a client organization, identifying the diversity-related issues that it needs to address, and developing a plan for it to address these issues. Its purpose, as for the previous exercise, is to examine the development of diversity plans for diverse organizations but this time from the consultant's perspective.

INSTRUCTIONS

1. Form groups of four to six members each to act as consulting firms.

2. Your consulting firm (select a name for yourselves) has received requests from several local organizations to provide help in initiating a diversity process. Each potential client says that its goal is to promote acceptance and appreciation of cultural diversity by its employees, whether the diversity is present in fellow employees, clients, or customers. However, you suspect that their motives for initiating a diversity process vary. The organizations that have requested your services include the following:

   a. a machine shop

   b. a bank

   c. the police force of a nearby town

   d. an elementary school

   e. a university

   f. a church

   g. a small marketing research firm

   h. a hospital

   i. a hospice

   j. a nonprofit social services agency

   k. a union of auto assembly workers

   l. a union of classified workers in state government

   m. the income maintenance department (in charge of programs related to welfare, food stamps, and so on) of the state government

   n. a country club that is trying to attract international tourists

   o. the chamber of commerce for a nearby town

   p. a mail-order company that sells clothing advertised in catalogs

   q. a large manufacturer of personal computers

   r. a retail department store in a nearby city

   s. a chain of retail boutiques that sell intimate apparel

Feel free to add to this list of potential clients based on your own interests or experiences.

3. As a group, decide who your client organization will be. (10 minutes)

4. Develop a diversity plan for your client organization. Begin by identifying the diversity issues that your client is most likely to face. The goal of the plan should be to promote attitudinal and behavioral change in how the organization and its employees respond to these issues. It should be designed to yield clear and measurable changes within a 6-month period. In preparing the plan, refer to the Possible Elements of a Diversity Process listed in the last exercise. (60 minutes)

5. Each group presents its diagnosis of the diversity-related needs of the selected client and its diversity plan. (10 minutes per group)

6. Participate in a class discussion based on the following questions: (remaining time)

   a. How do the consultants differ in their diagnoses of the diversity-related needs of their clients?

   b. How do the consultants differ in their involvement of the client in the design of a diversity plan?

   c. How well does each plan seem to respond to the unique situation in which it would be implemented? How could it be improved?

   d. What are the advantages and disadvantages for organizations in using outside consultants to initiate a diversity process? Under which organizational conditions would it be *best* to use consultants? *Worst* to use consultants?

Relating as Equals

Purpose:
1. To identify the qualities of egalitarian relationships between members of diverse groups.
2. To explore the behavioral patterns that *inhibit* the development of egalitarian relationships.
3. To explore the behavioral patterns that *enhance* the development of egalitarian relationships.

Preparation: Respond to the exercise questions.

Time: 90 to 120 minutes

INTRODUCTION   Madelyn Jennings (1993), a top executive of the Gannett Company, observed, "Homogeneous groups may solve problems faster, but diverse groups are more creative in their solutions." Diverse groups tend to avoid the pitfalls of "groupthink," common to demographically similar groups, whereby groups forgo critical thinking because they are preoccupied with maintaining a sense of cohesiveness. Also, as work groups become more tolerant of different points of view, their creativity and problem-solving abilities are increased and they are able to generate more and better ideas. As a result, organizations become more open to new ideas in general and are likely to be more responsive to changes in their operating environments (Adler, 1991, Chap. 5).

AUTHOR'S NOTE: This exercise was prepared by Mark Maier. It is reprinted from "The Gender Prism: Pedagogical Foundations for Reducing Sex Stereotyping and Promoting Egalitarian Male-Female Relationships in Management," in the *Journal of Management Education* (Vol. 17 No. 3, 1993, pp. 285-314). Used with permission.

However, the benefits of diversity cannot be achieved unless members of diverse groups are able to relate to each other as equals.

The purpose of this exercise is to consider what it will take for members of diverse groups to establish truly egalitarian relationships in the workplace. The two groups are specified in the instructions as women and men. However, as for Exercise 5, "Counteracting Group Stereotypes," the basic design of the exercise may be applied to workplace relations between any two groups that are in some way different from each other.

INSTRUCTIONS   1. Prior to class, write down your initial thoughts to these questions:

   a. Think of someone with whom you have had a relationship that you could characterize as "truly equal." How did you know it was equal? What qualities made it such?

   b. List the things that *members of the other sex* do in work situations that *inhibit* you from relating to them as equals.

   c. List the things that *you* do in work situations that *inhibit* the establishment and maintenance of egalitarian relationships between the sexes.

d. List the things that *members of the other sex* do (or could do) to *promote* the establishment and maintenance of egalitarian relationships.

e. List the things that *you* do (or could do) to *promote* the establishment and maintenance of egalitarian relationships.

2. In class, participate in a discussion of the qualities of egalitarian relationships, based on responses to the first question. (10 minutes)

3. Form two separate groups of women and men. Each group should have its own, preferably private, space in which to meet.

4. In your same-sex group, identify *inhibitors* of egalitarian relationships imposed by both sexes, based on responses to the second and third questions. (15 minutes)

5. Participate in a class discussion of how each sex contributes to the inhibition of egalitarian relationships. Groups' perceptions should be shared for all four quadrants of the following grid: (30 minutes)

	Male Group	Female Group
What Women Do		
What Men Do		

6. Form mixed-sex groups of 6 to 10 members.

7. In your mixed-sex group, identify *enhancers* of egalitarian relationships that are or could be promoted by both sexes, based on responses to the fourth and fifth questions. (15 minutes)

8. Participate in a class discussion of how each sex contributes (or can contribute) to the enhancement of egalitarian relationships. Groups' perceptions should be shared as follows: (remaining time)

   a. What women do (or can do).

   b. What men do (or can do).

REFERENCES

Adler, N. J. (1991). *International dimensions of organizational behavior* (2nd ed.). Boston: PWS-Kent.

Jennings, M. P. (1993, August). *Boundaries in the boundaryless organization: "The glass ceiling" phenomenon.* Symposium chaired by D. J. Cohen and delivered at the annual meeting of the Academy of Management, Atlanta, GA.

Gender and Diversity in the Workplace of the Future

Purpose:	1. To examine current trends in workplace relations between members of diverse groups.
	2. To speculate about what future workplace relations between members of diverse groups will be like.
	3. To identify personal actions that may be taken to bring about positive workplace relations in the future.
Preparation:	Read the two scenarios and respond to the questions that follow.
Time:	60 minutes

INTRODUCTION   Although changes in the demographic composition of the labor force have brought about changes in what it is like to work in today's organizations, it is a matter of debate as to how much the workplace has actually changed. Most people agree that there has been *some* change in workplace relations between members of diverse groups; however, whereas some see progress, others see preservation of the status quo. One observer in the late 1980s applied an old saying to male/female roles in the workplace: "The more things change, the more they stay the same" (Fuchs, 1988, p. 32). The purpose of this exercise is to encourage reflection about the changes that have already occurred in the workplace as a result of labor force demographics, speculation about the changes yet to come, and contemplation about the role that you can play in determining what the future changes will be.

INSTRUCTIONS   1. Prior to class, read the following two scenarios:

Scenario A

Virtually all organizations have been striving for some time to be multicultural in their management practices, and they have gone about as far as they can toward achieving this goal. Sex discrimination as well as discrimination on the basis of race, ethnicity, and other job-irrelevant characteristics has become taboo behavior in the workplace. Managers who practice such discrimination are subject to immediate dismissal or other punitive action. On the other hand, managers who find creative ways to take advantage of cultural diversity among their subordinates are rewarded. At the same time, equal employment opportunity laws are being rigorously enforced, and organizations that do not adhere to their dictates are putting themselves at considerable risk.

Organizations have made great strides in helping their employees to meet both their work and family needs. Couples have also been making personal trade-offs to enable both members to pursue their careers with equal satisfaction. As a result, family concerns are now having similar influences on the careers of both partners.

These changes have in turn affected the socialization experiences of children. Because their parents are leading more similar work lives, girls and boys are developing similar career aspirations and perceptions of the workplace. They see few barriers to their working in any career they would like to pursue.

With the resulting reduction in the sex segregation of occupations, most work groups now have balanced sex ratios. Male and female co-workers treat each other essentially as individuals, without regard to sex. Gender stereotyping in the workplace is a subject that has been relegated to books or articles about working conditions up until the latter part of the 20th century.

The proportions of women and minorities in management have become equivalent to their respective proportions in the labor force as a whole, a condition that primarily reflects individual goals rather than family or organizational constraints. The proportions at different levels of management are relatively balanced, with no sex, race, or ethnic group having a monopoly on the most powerful positions. Management styles that emphasize the needs of people as well as the need for task accomplishment are encouraged, because such styles are the best at eliciting employees' ideas and commitment.

Organizations are operating at peak performance levels because they are finally making the best possible use of all their available talent. They distribute monetary and other rewards equitably, and their employees are achieving maximum job satisfaction because they hold the positions that are best suited to their particular skills and interests.

Scenario B

Organizations pay lip service to equal employment opportunity laws, which are seen as more relevant to a distant past (if they were ever relevant then) than to the present and are generally not enforced. Affirmative action plans that are submitted to the government have no connection with the reality of the workplace and are not intended to be the basis for any real action. Organizations allow managers to take sex, race, ethnicity, and other personal characteristics into account in decision making if they believe that it is important. Top executives occasionally make speeches about the importance of equal opportunity and valuing cultural diversity and send out form letters on the subject to employees, but everyone knows that these are simply empty gestures.

Most organizations let their employees fend for themselves in satisfying their family needs. Work is assumed to be a good employee's primary concern, with family issues relegated to the home. Working couples slant decisions on the handling of household responsibilities in favor of the male, because his career is implicitly seen as more important than his partner's. This message is reinforced in the socialization experiences of children. Young girls and boys learn that, if a couple is forced to compromise on careers, the woman's interests will be subservient to those of her male partner.

The sex ratios of groups are heavily skewed in favor of either males or females depending on the occupation. Anyone who pursues an occupation that is atypical of his or her sex will probably achieve the unenviable position of being the only man or woman in the work group. Gender stereotypes are the primary basis for predicting and evaluating people's behavior.

Within the ranks of management, the proportions of women and minorities have stabilized at levels below their respective proportions in the labor force. The more powerful the position, the less chance a woman or minority group member has of holding it. There are very few women and minorities in the ranks of top management. A masculine management style, emphasizing attention to task accomplishment rather than the needs of people, remains the norm.

Organizations have not increased their productivity levels because they have not made any real changes in the use of their employees. Men continue to receive a higher share of monetary and other rewards than do women. Not surprisingly, men also report generally higher levels of satisfaction with their jobs and careers, whereas women report either frustration with or reluctant acceptance of the constraints placed by their families and organizations on their careers.

2. Write down your answers to the following questions:

   a. Which scenario best reflects today's realities? Why?

   b. Toward which scenario have we been heading in recent years?

   c. Which scenario will better represent reality 25 years from now?

   d. How can you personally contribute to bringing about Scenario A in your lifetime?

3. In class, participate in a class discussion based on the above questions.

REFERENCE   Fuchs, V. R. (1988). *Women's quest for economic equality*. Cambridge, MA: Harvard University Press.

About the Author

Gary N. Powell, Ph.D., is Professor of Management in the School of Business Administration at the University of Connecticut. He is the author of *Women and Men in Management,* now in its second edition (Sage, 1993), and is a nationally recognized scholar and educator on the subject. His graduate course on women and men in management won an award for innovation in education from the Committee on Equal Opportunity for Women of the American Assembly of Collegiate Schools of Business (AACSB). He also has won the University of Connecticut School of Business Administration's Outstanding Undergraduate Teaching Award. He has served as Chairperson of the Women in Management Division of the Academy of Management. He has published over 60 articles and presented over 60 papers at professional conferences. He has served on the Board of Governors and as Cochair of the Status of Minorities Task Force of the Academy of Management. He is a past president of the Eastern Academy of Management. He has served on the Editorial Boards of *Academy of Management Review* and *Academy of Management Executive.* He is a former project engineer and systems analyst with General Electric, having graduated from its Manufacturing Management Program. At GE, he designed and implemented automated project scheduling systems as well as systems for inventory control, production control, materials procurement, facilities management, and so on. He has provided management training and development for several companies, including GE-Capital, General Signal, Apple Computer, Monroe Auto Equipment, All-State, and CIGNA, and has conducted numerous other workshops. He received his Ph.D. and a master's degree in business administration from the University of Massachusetts and a bachelor's degree from MIT. He is a member of Beta Gamma Sigma, a business honorary association.